The
MORAL
FOOL

The
MORAL
FOOL

A CASE FOR AMORALITY

HANS-GEORG MOELLER

COLUMBIA UNIVERSITY PRESS

New York

Columbia University Press

Publishers Since 1893

New York | Chichester, West Sussex

Copyright © 2009 Columbia University Press

All rights reserved

Library of Congress Cataloging-in-Publication Data

Moeller, Hans-Georg, 1964–

The moral fool: a comparative case for amorality / Hans-Georg Moeller.

p.   cm.

Includes bibliographical references and index.

ISBN 978-0-231-14508-4 (cloth: alk. paper) —ISBN 978-0-231-14509-1

(pbk.: alk. paper) —ISBN 978-0-231-51924-3 (e-book)

1. Social ethics.   2. Moral conditions.   3. Social values.   I. Title.

HM665.M633   2009

171'.7—dc22

2008050513

Printed in the United States of America

c 10 9 8 7 6 5 4 3

p 10 9 8 7 6 5 4 3

CONTENTS

In my personal experience
the more seriously I tried to do good and to avoid evil,
the more clearly I realized myself to be far away
from good and to be involved in evil.
Masao Abe, *The Emptying God*

"God save us always," I said, "from the innocent and the good."
Graham Greene, *The Quiet American*

ACKNOWLEDGEMENTS

THE PRESENT BOOK IS very similar in content to a recent publication by Günter Wohlfart, a longtime colleague and friend. The title of Günter's book is *Die Kunst des Lebens und andere Künste: Skurrile Skizzen zu einem eurodaoistischen Ethos ohne Moral (The Art of Living and Other Arts: Ludicrous Sketches of a Euro-Daoist Ethos without Morality)* (Berlin: Parerga, 2005). He is currently working on another manuscript discussing similar issues. Its tentative title is "Moralphilosophische Splitter." In the notes I referred to Günter's work only a couple of times, but my whole approach toward Daoism, ethics, and philosophy in general has been shaped to a great extent by exchanges with and cooperation from Günter during the past fifteen years.

I am deeply indebted to Ryan O'Neill for agreeing to help me out again with my English. Ryan not only corrected many linguistic errors but also relentlessly cut what was mere repetition, what was not really necessary to say, and what was better left unsaid.

The following friends and colleagues read the manuscript in whole or in part and provided detailed criticisms and suggestions for changes: Hannes Bergthaller, Paul D'Ambrosio, Jay Goulding, John Maraldo, Franklin Perkins, Rolf Trauzettel, and Günter Wohlfart. I am also grateful to a number of students at Brock University who discussed with me the ideas presented in this book.

Many thanks to Anne R. Gibbons for her careful editorial work and her encouragement, and to Wendy Lochner and Christine Mortlock at Columbia University Press for their support and advice.

Finally, I thank Brock University for providing generous research funds.

This time, I asked my wife if, as is often seen in other books, she would like to be thanked in the acknowledgments. She said she did not really know what she should be thanked for and, instead, would rather have me give her my royalties.

The
MORAL
FOOL

INTRODUCTION | IS IT GOOD TO BE GOOD?

Es ist klar, dass sich die Ethik nicht aussprechen läßt.
(It is clear that ethics cannot be expressed.)

Ludwig Wittgenstein, *Tractatus Logico-Philosophicus,* 6:421

HARDLY ANY POLITICAL PURGE, religious war, or ethnic cleansing was not justified, embellished, or inspired by great moral values: justice, righteousness, freedom, liberty, equality, human rights—you name it. Robespierre, Hitler, and Pol Pot all acted in the name of virtue. When people kill each other, especially on a massive scale and in organized fashion, ethics are usually held in high esteem. It is much easier to murder a man if you believe that he is evil—and that you are good. Of course, the defenders of ethics will say: "Well, so what, no moral value is immune to abuse." But what is abuse? An ax can be used for cutting down an old oak tree that will keep your house warm in the winter. It can be used to split the skull of a criminal who attacks your family; it can be used to cut off the head of a man sentenced to death. It can be used to assassinate a tyrant. It can be used to kill your enemies in war. It can be used to break into a rich man's home. It can be used to torture a terrorist. It can be used to take deadly revenge. Where does its use end and its abuse begin? What are the rules for the use and the abuse of a tool? Who defines these rules, and when do they apply? Morality is a tool. It is not, unlike an ax, used for splitting things into halves, but for dividing people into two categories: the good and the bad. It is a rhetorical, psychological, and social tool. To say it can be used and abused is the same as to say: It is not guns that kill, but people. I do not believe in this logic. Axes and guns are not "innocent." The categories of innocence and guilt do not apply to tools.

This book does not say, Abolish morality! That would make as much sense as saying: Abolish all axes! (or guns, for that matter). But it does question the commonly held belief that morality is, in and of itself, a *good* thing. It is not. It is not more of a good thing than an ax or a gun. My main issues are Who says that morality is good? Why do people say this? How is morality used? And, Do the answers to these questions suggest that morality is inherently good? Are there different kinds of distinguishing between good and bad, and what kind of good/bad distinction is the moral one?

The goodness of morality normally goes unquestioned. But isn't it a circular argument to say that to distinguish between good and evil is good rather than evil? How can it be morally good to make such a distinction?[1] If it is, then moral goodness would paradoxically justify itself—or be simply evident. I think that the historical figures Robespierre, Hitler, and Pol Pot sufficiently demonstrate that morality is neither necessarily nor evidently good.

To say the opposite, that morality is evil, would be equally absurd. It would be just as absurd as saying that an ax or a gun is in and of itself evil. It would be as absurd as saying, "It is guns that kill, not people." The absurdity of one statement does not make its opposite necessarily truer. That axes or guns are not innocent does not make them guilty. None of these categories apply.

What I argue here is that one cannot say that morality is good or evil. Similarly, one cannot say that an ax or a gun is good or evil. I question the fundamental validity of such general ethical judgments. But my argument is not merely nihilistic. I also suggest that morality—or ethics—can be dangerous and that it may be advisable to be cautious with it. I say this because the idea is so often overlooked. In my profession, academic philosophy, interest in ethics has been, as in society on the whole, very much on the rise in recent years. If you want a job as a philosophy professor it is, nowadays, best to specialize in ethics: in the history of ethics, applied ethics, business ethics, bioethics, gender ethics—the list is growing all the time. Ethics are in vogue. Politics and the mass media are all concerned with ethics. Even the economy is nowadays supposed to consider ethical questions. And in every case it is presupposed that ethics are ethically good.

I do not think that ethics are ethically good or bad. I do not believe in inherent goodness or badness. But I believe that it is meaningless to speak of the abuse of a tool when it works perfectly well. Just as an ax chops wood as well as it can chop off heads, morality can be used equally well for helping or killing people. What was an ax made for? To say that it can be abused is to say that it was somehow created with only good uses in mind, and that later on someone found it could be used for bad ones as well. This is nonsense. What was the good intention behind the "invention" of ethics that was then later on, in some cases, perverted by sinister thugs? There is no goodness and badness in a tool, be it social or mechanical. Goodness and badness are always judgments, ascriptions by an observer. There is nothing inherently good or bad in an ax—and the same is true for ethics, in exactly the same sense.

Just like an ax, ethics can be deemed good or bad. It is clear that an observer can decide if a tool is being used well or not. But such a decision does not make ethics absolutely good or bad. Since, in our society, ethics are overwhelmingly observed as being good, I think it is important to point out the opposite, namely that there is equal reason to observe that ethics are bad. And therefore, it may be advisable to minimize the use of ethics. Again, the same could be said with respect to axes or guns.

But isn't it still paradoxical to say that ethics are bad? Isn't this, notwithstanding all disclaimers, itself an ethical proposition? The epigraph from Wittgenstein's *Tractatus* states that ethics are ineffable—and thus may seem paradoxical in a similar way. How can one *say* that something cannot be talked about? Wittgenstein discusses this issue in more detail in his "Lecture on Ethics."[2] His basic argument there is, in poetical terms, that if a book on ethics were possible all other books would "explode." If it were indeed possible to define what is truly good, what else of any significance would remain to be said? It would be such a fundamental revelation of truth that nothing else would matter. However, Wittgenstein explains, meaningful language is unable to perform such a superhuman task. Meaningful propositions relate to facts, and foundational ethical statements are not factual but, so to speak, ideal. The attempt to speak ethically is, according to Wittgenstein, an attempt to get beyond the confinements of meaningful language; it is like trying to get beyond the limits of language. We can say that a particular way leads to London, but not that this is *the* right way. There is no meaning attached to the rightness of a way in any absolute sense. Wittgenstein argues that, in the same way, ethical statements transcend factual linguistic meaning.[3]

To use the terms "good" and "bad" in a truly ethical way is to use them, for Wittgenstein, in an absolute way. To say this person is good—in a strong moral sense of the word "good"—is very similar to saying that this is *the* good or *the* right way to London. An amoral use of the terms "good" and "bad" is, for Wittgenstein, "relative." We may say: This person is a good runner, or a good mother, or a good friend. But this does not mean that we make an absolute ethical judgment about the person. She is a good mother to us—but that does not exclude the possibility of her being a criminal. To be good at sports means you are good at winning competitions and to be good at school means you get good grades. None of these usages of the word "good" is moral. It is by no means clear that winning in sports or having good grades is morally preferable to the opposite in all cases. The moral usage of the word "good" is only one of many other possible usages. One problem with the moral usage of the term "good" is that it leads to rather general statements. It never really says what is particularly good about the thing one is speaking of.

Neither people nor events are simply good or bad. They are usually, in some way or other, good for some and bad for others. When I say that ethics are not good, I mean this always in a specific and not in a general sense. An ethical mindset, for instance, can be psychologically unpleasant. An ethical work of art can be boring, and an ethical philosophy can be grotesque. An ethical war can lead to the killing and mutilation of many people who'd prefer not to be killed or mutilated. An ethical trial can be legally problematic, and so on. In this sense, ethical thought, ethical literature, ethical philosophy, ethical wars, and ethical justice can be deemed bad. But this does not mean that they are *immoral*. Perhaps wars, trials, and literature can be morally appreciated and justified. But, in an *amoral* sense, this ethical goodness does not necessarily translate into goodness in any concrete sense. The legal killing of a mass murderer may be morally just—but it is neither necessarily and *practically* good for the person who is going to be killed, nor for society, nor for the legal system. Perhaps there are a lot of advantages and benefits for criminals, society as a whole, and the judicial system if it avoids the use of a—perhaps—morally just penalty.

My position could be labeled "agnostic." It is a position that says that we cannot ultimately know if ethics are good or bad. Put a little more poetically, it is the position of the "moral fool." I derive this image—as I do my position on the whole—from Daoist philosophy and Zen Buddhism. But I also rely on a number of contemporary authors, most importantly the German sociologist Niklas Luhmann. There are many other modern Western thinkers on whom one can rely when criticizing ethics, among them the British writer John Gray. I refer to him and others as my argument unfolds. Here, at the beginning, I want to make clear that the moral fool is *not* a fundamentalist. If people are of the opinion that taking drugs is not necessarily a good thing, this does not necessarily mean that they think that all marijuana should be destroyed or that they never inhaled. They simply think that marijuana is potentially dangerous and that if one chooses to smoke it, one should be careful with it. The same is true for the amoral person with respect to ethics.

The moral fool simply does not understand why ethics are necessarily good. He does not know if the moral perspective is good at all. This does not mean that he is entirely without ethical judgments. The moral fool is not so different, I assert, from most people much of the time. Most of the time we neither think nor speak in ethical terms at all, and even when we do, we are often not entirely sure what exactly is, and what is not, ethical. The moral fool, I argue, is not at all an exemplar or an ideal; he is not an inverted ethical hero. To be a moral fool is actually quite common, and my point is that there is absolutely nothing wrong with this. In fact, I think that problems often arise when we try to overcome our moral foolishness. This book is thus written in defense of the moral fool. It is written to promote moral foolishness and its merits.

I do not believe that ethics can be identified as inherently good or bad. But this does not mean that we—and I include myself here—do not constantly distinguish between what we think is good or bad. But, like the moral fool, I am not convinced that this differentiation is necessarily a good thing. Also, I believe that most of our distinctions between good and bad are nonethical or amoral. Ethical distinctions, I argue, are an *extreme* type of distinguishing between good and bad—and thus, as it is often the case with extremes, rather dangerous. To argue that something is potentially dangerous or harmful is, I believe, not necessarily an ethical claim—and I do not mean it in an ethical sense. For example, to say that using axes or guns is dangerous does not imply that they are evil tools nor that those who use them are evil people. I do not even think that those

who use tools dangerously are evil. I think, however, they may well be criminal or mentally ill and should therefore not be allowed to use them and probably should be sanctioned if they do. Similarly, I do not think that making dangerous and harmful use of morality is necessarily evil. But I wouldn't be opposed to the idea of declaring those who use this communicative tool in a dangerous and harmful way to be criminal or mentally ill.

It would be entirely bizarre to advocate the elimination of the distinction between good and bad. But this does not imply that this distinction is always an ethical distinction. And it means even less that the distinction, as such, is good or bad. I argue that it is less dangerous and therefore potentially less harmful to use the good/bad distinction in an amoral sense. And I try to show what kind of concrete harm can be done when ethical categories abound—particularly in cases where they could easily be avoided.

Perhaps the two most important substitutes for ethics are "love" and "law." But these terms can easily be misunderstood. So I give a number of examples to illustrate right away how I use them in the context of my argument. The primordial work of literature that deals with love and law, as I understand these terms, is the ancient Greek tragedy *Antigone* by Sophocles. The crucial conflict depicted in the play is the following: Polynices, a young man from Thebes, is killed in battle *against* his home city in front of its gates. Creon, the ruler of Thebes, issues a decree that makes it illegal (by punishment of death) to grant this traitor a formal burial. Antigone, Polynices' sister, however, does not follow the law and, as Hegel says in his *Aesthetics*, "in the piety of her love for her brother, she fulfils the holy duty of burial."[4]

The most famous philosophical analysis of this narrative is in Hegel's *Phenomenology of Spirit*. Here, Hegel seems to use the story to illustrate a point that is quite the opposite of my own. For him, the story does not depict the "antidotes" of morality but rather the "dialectics" between what he calls ethics (*Sittlichkeit*), as represented by Antigone, and morality (*Moral*), as represented by Creon, that is, between two kinds of morality.[5] But upon closer inspection, and by also taking into account Hegel's own depiction of Antigone's position, one can discern a certain ambiguity in his interpretation. I side with an alternative amoral reading of the story that one may, paradoxically, also ascribe to Hegel and that has been nicely expressed by Walter Kaufmann: "[Hegel] realized that at the centre of the greatest tragedies of Aeschylus and Sophocles we find not a tragic hero but a tragic collision, and that the conflict is not between good and evil but between one-sided positions, each of which embodies some good."[6] In line with this, I prefer to read *Antigone* not chiefly as a collision between different kinds of moralities but rather as the conflict between two archetypal *amoral* perspectives.

For me, Antigone does not primarily illustrate, as for Hegel in the *Phenomenology of Spirit*, female obedience to divine law, but rather, as for Hegel in the *Lectures on Aesthetics*, a sister's *love* for her brother.[7] It is entirely irrelevant if Antigone finds her brother's actions morally acceptable or not. She looks at him not from a moral perspective, but as his *sister*. She buries him not because she appreciates what he did but because of her sisterly feelings. This meaning of love is what I have in mind here, and it is quite different from two perhaps more common uses of the term "love," namely unconditional *Christian* love (agape) or *passionate* love for a lover. Antigone was not a Christian. What she did for her brother, she would not have done for anyone else. She was not "in love" with him and felt no passionate (and sexual) desires for him. Christian love tends to be highly moral; it is prescribed by a religious doctrine or commandment: Love thy neighbor. Antigone does not follow such a divine command. Passionate love is normally quite amoral (but it can also easily be immoral). The problem with passionate love is that, if it is not pathological, it comes with an expiration date. To be "madly in love" is, normally (and fortunately), only a temporary state of mind and body. Antigone's love for her brother is not of this kind.

Creon does not act emotionally at all—or, at least, his emotions are irrelevant. He acts as someone whose function is to establish social order. Thus, *personal* considerations have to be ignored. He does not deal with Antigone as an evil person, but as someone who has violated the *law*. As was the case with Antigone and her brother, it is irrelevant what Creon thinks morally about Antigone. As someone who has to enforce the law, he cannot take into account Antigone's individual character. He has to punish her in order to make it clear that treason cannot be tolerated if Thebes is to survive.

Antigone thus demonstrates not the clash of two moralities, but the coexistence of two amoralities that, in *exceptional* circumstances, cannot be reconciled. Neither of these amoralities is more or less moral. There is no hierarchy between them. We cannot measure which one is, in any universal sense, ethically better. This is the tragic aspect of *Antigone*: It is not about a moral conflict, but about an amoral dilemma that cannot be solved "justly." It illustrates not the power but rather the *impotence* of morality. Similarly it does not illustrate the weakness of both amoral perspectives, but their respective strengths.

Morality can help neither Creon nor Antigone. But their antagonism arises only because of the extraordinary nature of the situation. In everyday life, both Creon's and Antigone's amorality function at the same time. As Kaufmann said, both of them are good—but not in the sense of the "good" in "good and evil." They are not absolutely good or right or just—which is why they can coexist normally with little conflict. When there is conflict it has the potential to become dramatic and tragic because there is no moral solution. This is why Sophocles depicts neither Antigone nor Creon as wrong. It would be wrong for Antigone, as a loving sister, *not* to love her brother (despite his moral shortcomings), and it would be equally wrong for Creon, as the ruler of Thebes, *not* to punish Antigone (despite her flawless character). It is tragic, but not sick.

On the contrary, a family dominated by ethics rather than love is somehow sick—and the same is true, on a much larger scale, for a society in which morality is supposed to trump the law. This simple fact was noted by Confucius. The *Analects* include the following dialogue: "The Governor of She in conversation with Confucius said, 'In our village there is someone called True Person. When his father took a sheep on the sly, he reported him to the authorities.' Confucius replied, 'Those who are true in my village conduct themselves differently. A father covers for his son, and a son covers for his father. And being true lies in this.'"[8]

I suggest that the moral of this little dialogue is not moralist—but, just as in *Antigone*, amoral.[9] True persons are not those who follow moral rules and publicly accuse their family members of wrongdoings. They will cover for their fathers and sons. And they do so, I argue, because they love them in a way similar to the way Antigone loved her brother. Prime Confucian virtues are "filial piety" (*xiao*) and "parental love" (*ci*). These are not grounded in any insight into moral principles, but in emotions. The "root" (*ben*) of all virtues is the feeling of love toward one's parents and one's siblings.[10] And it has to be established from birth. A child who grows up well will have this emotional root within herself and thus, in the Confucian model, be enabled to become virtuous. This means that all moral virtues are grounded in something amoral—in a feeling. Morality is not the root; the root is the natural attachment and emotional bond that grows between family members. For the Confucians, a healthy and moral society is not ultimately founded on moral principles and a rational (Kantian) grasp of one's duties but on the feelings that emerge within families. Morality is founded on something amoral—and this is why morality can never outweigh family feelings. The Confucian true person is one who has well cultivated his or her emotional roots and will therefore always naturally do what is appropriate and have no need to look for certain abstract principles or external authorities for guidance.

The Confucian dialogue also implicitly touches on the second antidote for morality, namely the law. Obviously, a society cannot be built on love alone. The Confucians were well aware that, unlike in the Christian model, it is not natural to love everyone. One normally loves one's spouse, one's parents, one's children, but not all others. To envision a society functioning on the basis of mutual love is quite unrealistic. The failure of religious and social movements (such as the flower power generation) that have tried to realize a society founded on love demonstrates this well enough. A family can function on the basis of love (instead of morality), but a larger society cannot. This does not, however, imply that ethics are the best foundation to provide for social harmony. A society needs to establish some rules and social mechanisms that prevent, for instance, the stealing of sheep. The tool that basically all complex societies have developed for dealing with such cases—outside of the family—is neither love nor morality, but the law. The law deals more coherently, more consequently, and even more rationally than morality with anything that is regarded as a crime in a society.

According to the Confucian view, love does not extend endlessly in society. Therefore other mechanisms are needed to establish social cohesion. The Confucians believed that rites could fulfill this function. From a contemporary perspective—and given the complexity and dimension of our society—it seems that legal procedures are more appropriate. Within a family, one does not need morality to love one another—but needs love to get along well. In a society one does not need morality to establish the law, but a legal system to prevent and deal with all sorts of "bad" behavior. I think it is perfectly in line with the Confucian perspective to say that a ritual or legal system can well accuse and sanction someone for steeling sheep. You just do not expect "sane" family members to sue one another. In a functional family, morality will not replace love, and in a functional society, ethics won't outplay the law.

Within the family, ethics are usually secondary in importance to love. We may condemn what our spouses, our children, our parents do. But since we love them, this condemnation does not normally result in a moral judgment. Even if we strongly disagree with what our loved ones do, we will, if they are really loved ones, not think of them as evil. This is the topic of John Steinbeck's novel *East of Eden*—and the famous film version of it with James Dean playing the unfortunate son Cal who yearns for the love of his father. Cal's father is a moral exemplar, he is always ethically right and just, he even forgives Cal all of his moral missteps. But in a crucial scene toward the end of the story Cal complains to his father that all his morality, including his forgiveness, does not make up for his inability to love Cal. The family portrayed in *East of Eden* is a dysfunctional family because ethics is substituted for love. This is not to say that an immoral family would be functional—but it demonstrates that ethical distinctions are not really what counts in a family. When love distinctions are replaced by ethical distinctions then the emotional harmony within a family is in danger. Children need to be loved even if they do things that are morally unacceptable. This is probably a rather commonplace insight, but I think it is still noteworthy since it is probably the most obvious case of ethics being potentially pathological.

Another contemporary version of the Antigone problem has been unfolding in Canada, and not in fiction, but in reality. Robert Latimer, a farmer from Saskatchewan, killed his twelve-year-old daughter who was suffering from severe disabilities that caused constant and incurable pain. The murder was labeled a mercy killing. Latimer acted in violation of the law in order to bring his daughter's terrible plight to an end. In accordance with the law, he was given a life sentence for second-degree murder. Just as in *Antigone*, the Latimer case illustrates a tragic conflict between love and law that *cannot* be resolved morally. The law allowed him to apply for limited parole after seven years of incarceration. In December 2007 his application was denied—and it was denied for moral reasons! The National Parole Board justified its decision by stating that Mr. Latimer had shown no "insight" into the nature of his crime. That is to say: he did not show any remorse. From a legal perspective, it was argued, so far to no avail, that the parole board acted against the law—which "requires the board to release an eligible inmate if he does not pose an undue risk to the community."[11] The board had imposed an impossible moral demand on Mr. Latimer: He was asked to admit that what he had done was not only illegal (which he never denied), but that it was also *immoral*. Mr. Latimer still felt that he had done the right thing based on his *love* for his daughter—and consequently did not publicly repent. He has now been convicted twice: Once, legally, by the court, and now, morally, by the parole board. I, for one, do not see the relevance of the moral conviction.

Even with respect to crimes that are morally much less ambiguous than that of Mr. Latimer, there is no obvious need for dealing with them ethically. One of the most infamous Canadian sexual serial killers, Paul Bernardo, committed his murders in the city where my university was located. In a public debate on religion that I had with a local pastor, the pastor argued that such heinous crimes as those of Paul Bernardo could only be condemned by referring to ultimate moral values and that these could only be derived from the Christian religion. Of course, I strongly disagreed. I believe that religion as organized and institutionalized morality is one of the more dangerous forms of ethics. But even the weaker version of my opponent's argument, namely that morality (and not necessarily religion) is needed to condemn terrible criminals is, in my view, flawed. Paul Bernardo was not apprehended by any moral group, but by the police. He was not judged and sentenced by a committee on ethics, but by a court. And he is not detained (for life) in an institution for the moral betterment of mankind, but in a prison. He was not even sentenced for his reprehensible character and his evil nature, but for the crimes he committed, for his violation of the law. While certain judgments about a person are usually taken into account in weighing the severity of a crime and the appropriate punishment— particularly with respect to the likelihood of reoffending—there is no law against being evil and no such law is needed. One can deal perfectly well with criminals such as Paul Bernardo by convicting them and locking them up. It is unnecessary to justify this with ethical reasons.

One actually has to commit a crime to be confronted with the law, and I think that this is good—good in a practical legal sense. We no longer engage in witch hunts. I also have to admit that I am happy to live in a country where there is a clear separation between the church and the law. I would certainly prefer not to be judged by a religious court if accused of a crime. Similarly, I am in favor of the separation of ethics and law (see chapter 8). I also would not like seeing people tried before ethical committees. In my view, the distinction between a purely ethical judgment of criminals and legal procedures parallels the distinction between a lynch mob and a court of law.

I think that within intimate personal relationships love (in Antigone's sense) functions better and less pathologically than morality. It has to be emphasized, though, that families in contemporary Western societies are very different from those in ancient Greece or in China. Accordingly, the notion of love that I am using here can also extend to, for example, stepparents or stepchildren. It can extend to longtime friends and to, basically, everyone with whom one has a very close bond. In today's society, the traditional family is often replaced by less clearly defined peer groups.

Admittedly, love does not extend very far, but contemporary society has developed a largely amoral function system, the legal system, which is quite effective in establishing and continuously modifying sets of rules that people more or less accept regardless of their individual moral convictions. While I advocate the law as a second antidote to morality, I do not wish to be interpreted as propagating some sort of law and order point of view. I understand the law *not* as an instrument of discipline but as a means that allows a society like ours to "stabilize expectations"—which is how Niklas Luhmann defines the function of the legal system.[12] For example, in most Western countries, traffic functions surprisingly well, given the number of cars, their speed, and the skills needed for safely operating a vehicle in various situations. This is achieved because traffic rules are largely followed; We know what to expect when we are on the road. This was not the case in earlier societies, and still isn't in many countries. We can expect that no one will go far above the speed limit, that no one will pass another car on a two-lane highway on a curve, that others will stop at a stop sign or a red light. Of course, accidents happen—mostly when such expectations are *not* met. They are the exceptions to the rule. In most cases, expectations are met, and thus our roads are *fairly* safe. Traffic does not function well because of traffic ethics and certainly not because of any type of love. It functions because of what could be called "law light."[13]

Traffic law is not draconian. No one goes to jail for parking in the wrong spot, nor even for speeding. Nor is it extremely strict. Most drivers, whenever possible, slightly exceed the speed limit. Most traffic violations remain without consequences. We do not usually get a ticket when we speed. The main function of the law in contemporary society is not to sanction and get rid of evildoers, but to provide a smooth playing field in a highly complex society. Traffic law is among the most effective laws in society, and it is also one of the least morally charged. People who drive recklessly are certainly not morally embraced, nor are they typically as morally condemned as murderers. Parking tickets and other minor offenses are generally laughed about, but this is not the case for most public misdemeanors, which are often regarded as shameful. Traffic law also does not involve any appeals to a higher justice. There is no just speed limit, and it is entirely arbitrary, or contingent, if one is supposed to drive on the left side of the road (as in Ireland) or on the right (as in Canada). Traffic rules are also subject to constant change. New signs are put up all the time; new regulations are put in place. These may even extend to aspects of traffic that were previously not legally regulated. It is quite conceivable that there will be traffic laws in the future that consider environmental damage. Perhaps it will become illegal to leave one's motor running while idling or to drive a car that uses gas inefficiently.

This is the idea of law that I have in mind throughout this book: law not (primarily) as an instrument of retribution, but as a social system that allows a complex society to be productive. In a lawless area, you do not know what to expect around the next corner, and this will prevent most people from ever going there. A functioning law light does not aim at preventing people from doing whatever they do, but at enabling them to do so. Such law is much more effective than a strict law and order approach that is highly charged with morality; it is much more effective than simplistic ethical appeals (would Jesus drive an SUV?); and it is not subject to any concept of fundamental and universal rights. Such law functions on an amoral basis, and the type of justice it operates with is not based on any divine or secular principles, but is rather quite similar to fairness in sport (see chapter 8).

It may be appropriate to classify my argument against ethics as pragmatic. I do not think that ethics are good in a pragmatic sense. In many cases, as I try to show, society works better with less ethics than with more. I discuss examples in law, art, and warfare. One of the standard arguments against pragmatism and a pragmatic concept of truth could possibly be brought forth against my position, namely, the accusation of relativism. It may seem that the moral fool is unable to come up with a solid evaluation of moral principles. It appears, with respect to ethics, that anything goes. Since he is unable to make a foundational judgment about what is good and bad—given some sort of pragmatic justification—basically every terrible deed can potentially be labeled "good." On the one hand, the moral fool lacks any basis for establishing moral principles, and, on the other hand, he is not in a position to morally condemn even the most obvious immoral acts.

I think that this is a rather shallow criticism. I counter it by referring to Richard Rorty, the most prominent American neopragmatist. When charged with the accusation of relativism with respect to his pragmatist concept of truth (that denies any form of objective truth), Rorty replied: "I do not see how a claim that something does not exist can be construed as a claim that something is relative to something else."[14]

Rorty was speaking about the concept of truth, not about ethics and moral concepts. (In fact, Rorty conceived of his pragmatism very much as an ethical philosophy.) Still, I believe that the same reply can be given to those who accuse the moral fool of ethical relativism. I address the issue of moral relativism in more detail and much more concretely in chapter 2, but it can be said here that the moral fool is someone who does not really see any basis for coming up with ethical principles. He does not understand on what grounds the absolute distinction between good and evil can be founded. This is to say, he makes the claim that something does not exist and does not claim that all moral principles are contingent upon certain circumstances. To be a moral fool and a moral relativist are two different things. The moral fool is, perhaps, more radical than the moral relativist because the latter is willing to accept at least the relative validity of moral principles.

Though a radical, the moral fool is not a hothead or fanatic. The position of the moral fool is one of modesty. He is perhaps, in a quite Socratic fashion, wiser than others by not thinking that he knows the answers to the most important problems.

The moral fool is also, in at least one important way, different from Wittgenstein's position in the "Lecture on Ethics." Wittgenstein points out at the end of his lecture that despite the total impossibility of stating anything that is, in an absolute sense, ethically meaningful, he still has the highest respect for such an endeavor. It seems that he saw it as something heroic—heroic in a tragic sense. As in the case of Sisyphus, the ethical effort will ultimately be futile, but nevertheless it constitutes, according to Wittgenstein, an essential aspect of our existence. The striving for ethics may be absurd, but it is a fundamental expression of what it means to be human.

I believe that the tragic ethical heroism that is so well depicted in Wittgenstein's lecture is representative of a Western and a humanist approach toward ethics. The moral fool is not a tragic hero. Unlike Wittgenstein, he does not value the effort of attempting to transcend boundaries, and he draws a very different conclusion from the insight into the ineffability of ethics. He is not really interested in the glory of failure—he is not interested in glory at all. The moral fool is, as I said, a rather modest fellow. He does not have great human aspirations and, consequently, does not fail in a grandiose way. The figure of the moral fool is derived from Daoism, and Daoism is not concerned with heroes. Furthermore, tragedy was not a genre that was of any significance in traditional Chinese literature or philosophy—it is practically absent in both. Daoism did not celebrate human ambition. It was not very enthusiastic about any human interference in nature to begin with. The moral fool is an ethical antihero, an Eastern alternative to the great and often tragic failure of human moralists in the Western tradition.

ON AMORALITY

ON AMORALITY

1 | THE MORAL FOOL

ONE OF MY FAVORITE Daoist stories is about the "old man at the fort." At first glance, it does not seem to have anything to do with ethical questions. Still, I believe that it is to be read, in the final analysis, as an allegory about what may be called the moralist mindset, and, if my reading is correct, that it presents a thoroughgoing as well as ironical and satirical criticism of such a mindset.[1] The story is quickly told. It is about an old "fool" who lives at a frontier fort and who cannot distinguish between good and bad. He loses his horse, and the other people call this bad, then the horse returns with a whole herd of horses, and the others call this good. His son then breaks a leg when riding one of the horses, and the others call this bad, but then the son is exempted from military service and thus survives a war, and the people call this good. One could, obviously, endlessly continue the story. On the surface, it is about good and bad luck. The old fool is too stupid to share his neighbor's conceptions of good and bad luck—but, of course, his foolishness turns out to be wiser than the common sense of the average people. Good and bad prove to be extremely shaky categories. One changes into the other, and the real fools are those who believe that they can judge the goodness and badness of things which, in fact, are subject to continuous change and reversal.

In my view, the story is not so much about the tricky nature of fate that so often makes events turn out different from what is expected. This is, for sure, an issue that the story plays with, but I don't think that it is at its philosophical core—if it were, the story would lack depth and merely express a rather commonplace truth. The story has, I think, a subtler message and this is primarily about the old man and his seemingly foolish inability to distinguish between good and bad. In other words, it's not so much about the shifting winds of change as it is about the human tendency to look at the world in terms of good and bad. When it comes to luck, we apply these labels quite naturally. Luck is always either good or bad. Only a fool can't see this. It can thus be said that the story addresses one of the most obvious cases of looking at the world in terms of good and bad—and it illustrates a stunning case of *not* thinking in these terms. How strange it is that the old man cannot even call *luck* good or bad!

Read in this way, the main point of the story is the foolishness of not deeming things good or bad—a foolishness that, paradoxically, emerges as wisdom. While luck is among the most obvious cases in which we apply the terms good and bad, morality is probably among the most severe and critical. With respect to luck, there is something playful in judgments about good and bad. If it's just bad *luck*, we may be able to laugh about it—at least later on. Moral judgments are not funny. To deem somebody morally bad is hardly a laughing matter. If we really feel that someone is morally bad, this is usually both a very strong and a very serious feeling. There is even a special term for this kind of badness: it is called "evil." Evil is the severest kind of badness and does not leave much room for humor or ambiguity.

I think that the foolishness of the old man at the fort is a very radical one. The case of good and bad luck is only meant to demonstrate his general mistrust of such a perspective. The old man simply lacks these categories. Ultimately, and in the most serious dimension, this implies that the old man is also, and most importantly, a *moral fool*. If he does not understand the difference between good and bad luck, he will not understand why or how people can make ethical distinctions. He will be blind with respect to moral judgments. It is this position that I defend in this book. I share the old fool's mistrust in the goodness of distinguishing between good and bad—particularly when it comes to morality and ethics. And I suggest that perhaps such moral foolishness may turn out, just as with the old man at the fort, as wiser than apparent moral cleverness and the beliefs and assurances that result from it.

So what do I have in mind when I talk about ethics and morality—and advocate being suspicious of them? Very much in line with my reading of the story of the old man at the fort, I conceive of them as ways of distinguishing between good and bad, and, more precisely, as probably the most serious or extreme form of this distinction. Ethically, the distinction between good and bad becomes the distinction between good and evil. In other words, the most uncompromising application of the terms "good" and "bad" is their ethical application. In its moral guise, this distinction applies to people and what they do and are, and to mark the degree of disdain that usually goes along with the negative side of this distinction.

When we say that an object is good or bad, it does not make sense to use the word "evil." We rarely accuse our car of being evil when it won't start on a cold day—and if we do, we do so jokingly or metaphorically. A judgment that concerns a car cannot really be a moral judgment since it lacks the capacity to be viewed ethically. The same is true for animals. We do not hold the skunk morally responsible for the bad odor it leaves behind, and normally we do not even pass moral judgment on a bear that kills someone, even though we may agree it has to be shot to prevent it from inflicting further harm. We do not kill the bear because it is evil, but because it is dangerous. There are also some human beings whom we do not think about in moral terms. A crying baby may well cause frustration and anger—even if it's one's own child—but what normal person would say that the child is evil? We also do not accuse people who lie in a coma and cost the taxpayer (at least in Canada) possibly hundreds of thousands of dollars of being immoral parasites. In all these cases we do not apply our moral mindset—and I think that this is, quite obviously, a practical thing. Who would want to live in a world where skunks that smell, children who cry, and costly patients are deemed evil? The moral use of the distinction good/bad seems to be an *extreme* form of this distinction that is not used in many—perhaps not even in most—cases. The question is, Is this extreme form of distinguishing between good and bad really desirable?

It is necessary to get a better understanding of exactly where the extreme of moral judgments lies. Moral judgments—moral applications of the good/bad distinction—normally have to do with social agency. Outside of a social context, morality does not have a place.

But even within society there are morality-free zones, so to speak. Infants and unconscious people, for instance, do not fully qualify as moral agents. One of the most famous and influential positions in modern Western moral philosophy, Kant's *Critique of Practical Reason*, points out with utmost clarity that an action as such does not have a moral quality, but only the *will* behind it. It is the intention and the motivation that can be called ethically good or bad. Infants and unconscious people may do things that are bad, but they cannot be evil because they do not have what we normally call free will. A moral judgment thus seems to presuppose not only social agency but also, and more specifically, human will and reason. If one has neither will nor reason then she cannot be judged in moral terms.

If, on the other hand, one has will or reason, one becomes morally responsible. This puts a heavy moral burden on humans, particularly in the Christian tradition. God has supplied us with free will—but this gives us the capacity not only to do wrong but also, in moral terms, to do evil, and, in religious terms, to "sin." In fact, if one believes in Christian doctrine, one faces the problematic inheritance of original sin. God created us as moral beings and we cannot escape our moral frailty and weakness. From a Christian perspective it is very difficult not to conceive of humans in moral categories. In a certain sense, Kant merely secularized the Christian ethical tradition. Being equipped with free will and reason, we cannot avoid our moral responsibility. We are inherently and inescapably moral. Neither Christianity nor Kantian philosophy allows for a nonethical understanding of human beings. Or, put positively: From both a Christian and a Kantian perspective, morality can be defined as the specific and exclusive capacity of humans (who have free will and reason) to be good or bad.

Morality or ethics is, accordingly, a very peculiar human trait. Its extremism lies in its being restricted to humans, and, more precisely, to a specific range of human beings. Nonhuman beings cannot be moral. But there are also human beings who cannot be moral, for instance, the previously mentioned infants and unconscious patients. These are, according to a moralist kind of logic, at the fringes of humanity. We may well love our little children or our demented grandparents, but since we do not look at them as moral agents, they are either not yet or no longer fully responsible members of society.

Moral capacity and a concept of mature humanity seem to be closely connected. Morality seems to have something to do with a conception of human life that focuses on free will and reason and a certain view of what it means to be an adult. It is a concept of good and bad that is reserved for those who fulfill the criteria of rational human individuals. As such, it reveals itself as an extreme form of humanism, since it applies only to humans, and, furthermore, only to those humans who are deemed fully human.

Another aspect of what it means to be morally good or bad—as opposed to being good or bad in a nonmoral sense—is that such a judgment has far-ranging consequences; it is, again, an extreme type of judgment. We reserve it for rational humans, but, of course, not all good/bad evaluations of responsible adults are ethical. If someone is, for instance, good at sports or at driving, this does not count as a moral quality. Moral judgments normally do not apply to specific abilities or achievements. As Kant noted, they do not apply to acts or performances at all. According to him, they only apply to the will behind an action, but perhaps even this definition is not sufficiently exact. When we call someone morally good or evil, I would argue, we normally do not refer to the person's specific intentions but to their *character*. If we say that a person is good, and we mean it in a moral sense, then we believe that he or she is *essentially* nice. We like or dislike not their will but them as an entire person. Moral judgments are in this sense unlimited; they do not refer to this or that quality. Instead, they refer to the general character of a person. Moral judgments tend to be fundamental. If we say that a woman is a bad runner, we do not say much about her. If, however, we say that she is evil, then it will not matter how good a sprinter she is. Saying "she is a good teacher, but a lousy cook" is very different from saying "she is a good teacher, but she is morally reprehensible."

By saying that morality is an extreme and perhaps the most serious form of the distinction good/bad, I also mean that it is reserved for those whom we consider to be fully human, and that it applies to them in a very essential way. Moral judgments only apply to those whom we take seriously (not to things and animals, not to infants or the senile), and it applies to them sweepingly.

At this point it is probably appropriate to further clarify the meaning of "morality" in relation to "ethics." Here I use both terms, as is common in contemporary English, more or less interchangeably. This makes sense since the two terms used to have the same meaning, one derived from ancient Greek (ethics) and the other from Latin (morality). Both the Greek and the Latin term designated behavior that was in line with what was socially accepted as "good." To be ethical or moral meant to act in a way that was considered proper, customary, and right. Accordingly, ethics and moral philosophy were similar disciplines that tried to define what constituted proper and right behavior, to identify the underlying principles of what was right and proper, and to establish norms that would provide guidance for acting in a righteous and appropriate manner. These disciplines also investigated what made someone virtuous and what virtues were, that is, what constituted the personal ground for being ethical or moral.

In modern Western philosophy several attempts have been made to distinguish terminologically between ethics and morality and thus to go beyond the traditional synonymy of the two terms. I briefly discuss three representative attempts. In the early nineteenth century Hegel—in the context of criticizing Kant's moral philosophy—introduced a peculiar distinction between ethics and morality. Ethics in Hegel's German is *Sittlichkeit*—which corresponds to the Greek and Latin meaning of ethics and morality explained above. Literally, *Sitten* are the customs and manners of behavior considered proper in a society. *Sittlichkeit*, or ethics, therefore means for Hegel "established custom, not a set of principles. *Sittlichkeit* is shared activity, shared interests, shared pleasures; it is not first of all, and perhaps not at all, rational reflection on the rules." This means: "The key to understanding *Sittlichkeit* is the notion of a *practice*. A practice or set of practices might have a set of explicit rules (as in chess or music composition) but it need not have any such rules."[2] Ethics, for Hegel, then means what is actually considered good behavior in a community. It is what, in the double meaning of this term, is *realized* as the good life in a community. As Charles Taylor has pointed out, ethics refers to the standards of good behavior and obligations that are "already there in existence," and thus with respect to ethics "there is no gap between what ought to be and what is." In Hegel's understanding, the opposite is the case with morality. Morality refers to the norms that we can intellectually define. If ethics refers to the "established custom," then morality means the "set of principles" that we may be taught, but that are not necessarily practiced in the community. It is what we can rationally accept and understand as being good, but what we do not normally experience in the community on a day-to-day basis. Taylor explains this meaning of morality: "Here we have an obligation to realize something which does not exist. What ought to be contrasts with what is. And connected with this, the obligation holds of me not in virtue of being part of a larger community life, but as an individual rational will."[3] Ethics is thus contrasted with morality. The former is the practice of customary goodness in society whereas the latter means a set of normative rules that one can arrive at through rational deliberation but that is not necessarily actualized.

The German social theorist Niklas Luhmann (1927–98) worked with a distinction between ethics and morality that is remarkably different from Hegel's use of the two terms. Luhmann defines "morality" as a type of communication by which the esteem or disesteem of others is distributed. Like his one-time teacher Talcott Parsons, he distinguishes between esteem and approval. Similar to my understanding of the moralist mindset as an extreme form of labeling people good or bad, Luhmann argues that moral judgments always concern the person as a whole. Approval is limited to certain acts or performances of a person and is therefore not a moral evaluation. We may approve or disapprove of one's decision or one's dress, but this is not yet a moral judgment. If, however, we esteem or disesteem people, then we either morally accept or disdain them. Moral distinctions distinguish between those whom we accept and those whom we don't. Accordingly, moral values are the criteria by which we either esteem or disesteem others. For Luhmann, morality is the condition of the market of social esteem.[4] Morality is neither customary behavior nor a set of principles, but the actual social differentiation between those who are deemed good and those who are deemed bad or evil. Whenever we qualify someone as "evil" we engage in moral communication. Morality is thus a social technique for introducing distinctions. It is a way of dividing our world into goodies and baddies. "Ethics," on the other hand, has a very specific meaning. Luhmann conceives of ethics as the theoretical reflection on morality. Ethics is therefore not moral, but, so to speak, metamoral. It is the nonmoral analysis of how morality works. Ethics is thus not concerned with actually determining who or what is either morally good or bad, but with explaining how morality works in society. Ethics is the science of morality that observes morality. It does not distribute esteem or disesteem but reflects on the fact that such distribution takes place and plays a major role in social life. Ethics is the sociological discipline that investigates moral communication.

A third attempt to distinguish between ethics and morality is that of the contemporary postmodernist thinker Drucilla Cornell. In her book *The Philosophy of the Limit* she writes:

> For my purposes, "morality" designates any attempt to spell out how one determines a "right way to behave," behavioral norms which, once determined, can be translated into a system of rules. The ethical relation, a term which I contrast with morality, focuses instead on the kind of person one must become in order to develop a nonviolative relationship to the Other. The concern of the ethical relation, in other words, is a way of being in the world that spans divergent value systems and allows us to criticize the repressive aspects of competing moral systems.[5]

In her understanding, "morality" is some sort of strict and relatively coherent normative system. It is like a definitive guidebook on how to act. To be "ethical" has a much more personal meaning for Cornell. It is a project of personal cultivation that enables one to engage in nonaggressive and tolerant relationships with others. Whereas morality results in a specific set of beliefs and rules, to be ethical is something entirely different. It is not used to judge others and oneself according to a rigid catalog of values, but works to live and coexist with others regardless of their specific identities.

All three terminological distinctions—Hegel's, Luhmann's, and Cornell's—make sense. The problem is that none of them correspond to the actual usage of the terms "ethics" and "morality" in contemporary English. The introduction of such a distinction therefore is, in each case, slightly artificial and forced. The authors give very good reasons for their respective understanding of the terms, but none of them have succeeded in making their definitions commonly accepted. In order to avoid adding another technical distinction between the words "ethics" and "morality," I have decided to simply follow their traditional synonymy. For me, ethics and morality are basically identical, and, accordingly, ethics and moral philosophy are the same discipline.

It has to be acknowledged, however, that while ethics and morality are more or less interchangeable terms in contemporary English—just as they once were in the Western philosophical tradition—their meaning has shifted since the time of ancient Greece and Rome. Very much in line with Hegel's concept of *Sittlichkeit*, the terms originally referred to what was considered good behavior in the sense of being in line with social customs and manners. Given the increase in the complexity of social life, the entirely new dimensions of multiculturalism and globalization, the new lifestyles brought about by the industrial and technological revolutions, the role of manners and customs has greatly changed since the time of Aristotle or Cicero. It is therefore no longer the case that ethics and morality primarily refer to what is generally regarded as socially proper, simply because it would be very difficult to actually identify what this is in today's world. In the ancient world it was, for instance, believed that a certain way of life was proper for all women—and that this way of life differed significantly from that of all men. Hardly anyone in the modern West would agree with such an understanding of morality and ethics. In correspondence with the drastic social changes that have occurred since the classical age, ethics and morality have taken on a different meaning. They are conceived not so much in terms of customs or manners but with personal integrity and individual character traits, on the one hand, and supposedly universal values such as justice, freedom, and equality, on the other.

Since it is not my intention to come up with a new ethics, I am not at all concerned here with defining the moral virtues or ethical norms of our society. I leave this to the moralists and professional ethicists. My intention is to bring forth a criticism of morality, not as a criticism of specific values or forms of behavior, but as a criticism of the moralist mindset. I question whether the moralist perspective is appropriate. Is it really necessary and good to look at the world in ethical terms? Is it advisable to make ethical judgments? Is it fruitful to think and talk in ethical terms? And, most of all: Is it helpful to deem others good or evil?

I am concerned here with the function of ethical distinctions in our society. In what follows, I analyze what happens when we heavily engage in ethical communication, with a special concern with the law and mass media. I understand ethical thought and communication as an extreme and highly serious form of distinguishing between good and bad that normally applies to persons and their acts. Of course, ethical reasoning can also be extended to groups of persons and collective acts. A war, for instance, can be deemed just or unjust and thus conceived of in ethical terms. But even in such a case it is usually assumed that some people are responsible for the war and that the morality or immorality of that war is ultimately the morality or immorality of those people. The same is true for politics. When it is said that certain policies are immoral it normally means that the regime that is responsible for these policies is in violation of ethical norms.

Being interested in the functioning of moral communication in our society and being a critic of morality, I mainly focus on the pathology of ethics. My attitude is thus somewhat similar to Nietzsche's.[6] I try to point out the disadvantages of moral distinctions and the specific pains and troubles that they create. This should not be confused, however, with advocating immorality. If a doctor advises her patient to stop smoking this does not mean the she advises him to do the exact opposite. There is, in fact, no positive opposite to smoking. The alternative to smoking is to stop smoking, and not to "do" its opposite. Similarly, the advice to be cautious with morality only advises one to be cautious. The moral fool is precisely not a moralist, but he is neither an immoralist nor a reversed moralist. To say that it is not necessarily good to be moral is not itself a moral judgment—as I point out in the introduction. The moral fool does not even claim that it is, in a strong sense, good to be amoral. A doctor would not say that it is, in a strict sense, healthy not to smoke. Refraining from smoking does not make you healthy; it simply eliminates a certain risk. In the same way, the moral fool refrains from taking the risk of making judgments about what is good or bad. But this does not imply that avoiding this risk makes you automatically good. Therefore, the moral fool does not say that it is morally good not to be ethical. He only says: I do not understand why some people seem so determined to look at the world in moral terms.

2 | NEGATIVE ETHICS

IN A BOOK ON negative ethics, the Swiss philosopher Hans Saner distinguishes four ethics of this type:

1. a radical renunciation of morality as a result of, for instance, a disgust with ethics and its failures,
2. a normative ethics that assumes that the good as such cannot be determined and that it therefore can only be explained negatively—analogous to the attempts of negative theology to define God,
3. a skeptical approach toward ethics that assumes that no general ethical guidelines or principles can be established since morality is always concrete and embedded in particular situations, and
4. an ethics that does not believe in the primacy of action but rather in the primacy of refraining from intervention—and that thus advocates an ethics of "letting-be."[1]

It may seem that the point of view of the moral fool is closest to the fourth type of negative ethics listed above. After all, this fool is a Daoist, and the Daoists came up with the maxim of "doing nothing (so that nothing remains undone)"—*wu wei* in Chinese. They advocated a lifestyle of noninterference that included ethical abstinence and conceived of the ethical mindset not as the solution to, but rather as an integral part of, social problems. I suggest, however, that the Daoist view—and my own, as it is derived from Daoism—is closer to the first type of negative ethics identified by Saner. But, instead of a disgust with ethics, I prefer to speak of a thoroughgoing distrust. The moral fool is unwilling to look at the world on the basis of ethical distinctions since he does not accept their validity. But this perspective does not exclude the other three types of negative ethics. The position that I present here is closest to the first type, the renunciation of the ethical perspective as unwarranted, unnecessary, and often unhelpful, but it certainly includes aspects of the other three. It is critical of attempts to establish a positive ethical system (see chapter 6); it certainly believes that good deeds are a matter of practice rather than of principles (see chapter 3); and it holds that minimizing human intervention is the best strategy (see chapter 7). The most radical aspect of moral foolishness still remains the attempt to deconstruct the moral framework.

A common criticism that has been brought forth against Daoism—and that can certainly be expected to be raised against my version of negative ethics—is that it is relativist. Given the renunciation of moral values, it seems that we lose the capacity to distinguish between good and evil. After denying the existence of ethical principles, it seems that anything, and everything, is allowed. If we embrace moral foolishness, how will we be able to condemn mass murder or genocide, and how will we be able to praise exemplary people who really make a difference in the world? Doesn't the moral fool make any ethical judgment relative in the sense of being ultimately arbitrary and groundless? If there are no objective moral standards, it seems that even the most terrible acts can be justified.

My point of view is that the moral fool is not a moral relativist but a critic of moral relativism. I argue that this type of negative ethics does not lead to relativism but, on the contrary, deconstructs moral relativism more thoroughly than most positive ethics do. I rely on ancient Daoist sources to prove this point. Instead of advocating any type of ethics, including a relativist one, the moral fool is suspicious of *all* ethics, including relativistic ones. Regardless of whether the ethical mindset is relative or universal, it is the ethical outlook that is problematic. The issue is not that one should limit the scope of one's ethical claims, but that it is dangerous to think and talk about the world in ethical terms at all.

The *Zhuangzi*, like many other ancient Chinese texts, frequently discusses moral distinctions by contrasting the great moral exemplars Yao and Shun (the ancient rulers) with the villains Zhou and Jie (the cruel tyrants who brought about the downfall of their dynasties). Mentioning these names today leaves us emotionally untouched, but in the historical context of ancient China they were highly charged with moral sentiment. The allusive power that was attached to these names might be compared with what is experienced nowadays when, say, Nelson Mandela and Adolf Hitler are mentioned. We are expected to feel some sort of awe when we hear the first name and, contrarily, some kind of outrage when we hear the second. We are brought up in a society that thus divides and cultivates moral judgment, and I can only assume that similar mechanisms, though tied to different models, were in place in ancient China. I draw this parallel to highlight the radicalism and provocative nature of the following quotation from the *Zhuangzi*: "Examining them in terms of inclinations, if assuming a standpoint from which it is right you see it as right, not one of the myriad things is not right; if assuming a standpoint from which it is wrong you see it as wrong, not one of the myriad things is not wrong. When you know that sage Yao and tyrant Jie each thought himself right and the other wrong, the commitments behind the inclinations will be perceived."[2]

What the *Zhuangzi* says here is as simple as it is shockingly true. From their own perspective and within the context of their respective environments, there is no difference in the moral evaluation of a Yao and a Jie. In other words, Adolf Hitler was, during the time of the Nazi regime in Germany, just as morally cherished as Nelson Mandela was morally condemned in South Africa under apartheid. Of course, we see things differently today, but we only do so by assuming our current moral perspective. What the *Zhuangzi* points out is that there is never a moral perspective devoid of context. Just as vigorously as we now believe in the moral goodness of Nelson Mandela and in the immorality of Adolf Hitler, many (white) people in South Africa and Germany during their respective times believed the opposite. Is the *Zhuangzi* therefore saying that there is no actual distinction between a Yao and a Jie, or between a Mandela and a Hitler—and is it therefore advocating an absolute moral relativism? I do not think that this is the case.

What the *Zhuangzi* implies is actually not a relativist standpoint, but a subtle criticism of such a point of view. Let us take a closer look. A relativist position, if taken seriously and in a positive manner, would state that moral judgments are always relative to their social and ideological context—and therefore acceptable within their contexts. So, taken to the extreme, this position would have to admit that, given the respective contexts, a Jie was just as morally good as a Yao, and a Hitler just as morally good as a Mandela. The *Zhuangzi* says that this is where the problem lies. The problem is not so much that all moral judgments are relative to a context—the *Zhuangzi* does not deny this—but that these judgments are held so dearly within their respective contexts that they may lead to all kinds of moral beliefs and, possibly, destructive deeds. It is a fact for the *Zhuangzi* that once, during Jie's time, Jie's morality was as strongly held to be right, as now, for the Confucians, it is Yao's. The *Zhuangzi* strongly cautions against such relativist beliefs. When acting on moral beliefs, one should be aware that other perspectives are always possible and that at other times people may have other views. People who heard the name Adolf Hitler once felt the same intensity of moral awe that we feel nowadays when we hear the name Nelson Mandela. We should therefore be cautious about inferring from *any* moral awe a right to act in a certain manner. Moral awe is always relative and can, possibly, be used to justify heinous acts. There is no guarantee whatsoever that the moral awe felt for the name of Yao may not turn out to be as disastrous as the moral awe felt for the name of Jie—and the same holds today for Nelson Mandela and Adolf Hitler.

The *Zhuangzi* therefore states that all moralist vigor, whether it be relativist or universal, is dangerous and potentially harmful. In some cases, as in the case of Jie, it turns out to be truly catastrophic, while in others, as in the case of Yao, it is, although relatively harmless in its outcome, still equally misguided. If one begins to look at the world and oneself in moral terms, this is already a turning away from the Dao. An allegory in the eighth chapter of the *Zhuangzi*, mentioned in the context of comparisons between villains and moral sages, explains this quite nicely: "Two boys, Zang and Gu, were together minding the flock, and both lost their sheep. When they were asked what happened, it turned out that Zang had brought a book to study, Gu had been idling away the time tossing dice. The two boys had dissimilar occupations, but in losing their sheep there was nothing to choose between them."[3]

There is a distinction between reading books and tossing dice—the one is considered a virtue, the other a vice—but the sheep are lost in any case. The loss of sheep is a metaphor for losing one's not yet morally spoiled nature. By self-righteously believing in one's moral superiority one loses one's amoral innocence, regardless of whether one does harm to others or not. Morality is not the solution to social problems—it is, instead, in the *Zhuangzi* (as well as in Nietzsche's *Twilight of the Idols*) among their causes.[4] A similar point is made in the following passage: "Formerly when Yao governed the world he made everyone exultantly delight in nature, which is excitement; and when Jie governed the world he made everyone suffer miserably in his nature, which is discontent. To be excited or discontented is to go counter to the Power [*de*]; and nothing in the world which goes counter to the Power can last for long."[5]

It is not the case that in effect Yao and Jie are the same—but they do give rise to some kind of moral sentiment. Nobody knows what can come out of moral sentiment once it is introduced. Experience shows, however, that more often than not, social crises and wars go along with a high level of moral conviction and emotionality on one or both sides. Once unleashed, emotions tend to increase and fuel themselves. The *Zhuangzi* thus states that after Yao the world became "agitated by restless ambitions, and only after that . . . you had the conduct of robber Zhi on the one hand and of Zeng and Shi on the other."[6] Robber Zhi, the shrewd outlaw of ancient China as well as Zeng Zi, the disciple of Confucius, and Shi Yu, a moral exemplar praised by Confucius (in *Analects* 15.7), are the results of the introduction of morality into society. The point here is that if the notion of good is introduced, it necessarily occurs within the context of a good/bad distinction—which may create problems that did not exist as such prior to the making of this distinction. In this way, morality creates the distinction between the good and the bad and subsequently allows for harmful applications of the distinction.

That feelings of righteousness turn out to be good for society is merely by chance. The opposite is equally likely and, in the long run, unavoidable. From good, to bad, to evil—so runs the sequence of the evolution of morality. The *Zhuangzi* thus concludes: "I am inclined to think that sagehood and knowledge are the wedges of the stocks and the cangue, that Goodwill [*ren*] and Duty [*yi*] are the pin and hole of fetters and manacles. How do I know that Zeng and Shi are not the whistling arrows which signal the attack of tyrant Jie and robber Zhi?"[7]

A society in which moral discourse prevails already shows the symptoms of moral disaster. The moral righteousness felt by the good Zeng and Shi might well turn into what was felt by the evil Jie and Zhou. The outcome is different, but the feeling is indistinguishable. Actions performed self-righteously always feel right to the self that performs them. People commit genocide not because they believe that it is immoral, but for the exact opposite reason. Hitler and his henchmen believed they were doing the right thing and that they did the world a great moral service. Therefore, the *Zhuangzi*, says, sages will rid themselves of moral feelings. Once contaminated with morality, it will be difficult to restrain oneself: "Rather than praise sage Yao and condemn tyrant Jie, we should be better off if we could forget them both and let their Ways enter the transformation."[8] Or, as one of the many depreciative statements about the important Confucian virtues at that time—perhaps comparable to moral values such as justice and liberty today—puts it: "Goodwill and Duty are the grass huts of the former kings; you may put up in them for a night, but not settle in them for long."[9] The Daoist sage in the *Zhuangzi* is amoral—and avoids being infected with morality whenever possible.

The specific problem with ethics is—and this is my first hypothesis—that it can lead to pathological states. It potentially leads to dangerous one-sidedness, or to put it in Western terms, self-righteousness. If one starts to conceive of oneself and others in ethical terms, then one is easily driven to look at the world in terms of black and white, of friends and enemies. The *Zhuangzi*—and Daoist philosophy in general—does not intend to blur distinctions that, after all, constitute the world and its changes, but instead tries to find a way to harmonize what is distinct. Ethical distinctions, however, pose a serious threat to the harmonious coexistence of that which is distinct. If one conceives of oneself and others merely as different or even opposite, this is not necessarily antagonistic. If, however, distinctions become ethical distinctions, then the possibility for conflict looms. The *Zhuangzi*'s and the Daoists' concern with ethics is that it transforms fruitful and productive distinctions into destructive hostilities.

Instead of advocating a relativist mindset, the *Zhuangzi* argues for an *amoral* stance—which is quite different. The *Zhuangzi* does not so much deal with the question of whether relativism or nonrelativism represents the attitude of the sage, but how he or she deals with morality. And the answer is rather clear. The sage is neither moral nor immoral but tries to rid herself of moral conceptions. This lack of moral distinctions is equated not with being blind to the differences in the world, but with being able to view these from a nonmoral perspective—or to use a term that I have used elsewhere, from the zero-perspective.

The underlying problem of moral distinctions is, I think, that they are not factual distinctions. They are distinctions based on value judgments, distinctions based on personal biases and interests. The Daoist sage has no biases and no interests; he has no agenda. Ethical judgments result from taking a position that imposes a certain *interpretation* on reality. Moral categories are not essential, but are added to acts and events. They are always the result of appropriating facts for the benefit of one's own worldview. By describing something in moral language one can either aggrandize one's own behavior or put someone else's down. Moral language is combative and it serves to justify one's self, condemn others, or both. It is always rhetorical and acts as a semantics that exploits facts or deeds in order to put oneself in a better light.

The obvious counterargument to what I just said is, Aren't there heinous crimes, for example, that call for an immediate moral reaction, that inevitably ask for moral disapproval? One may think of the 9/11 attacks for instance. Don't we have to respond to such crimes with moral outrage? This may be an immediate reaction, but it is, I dare say, not the position of the Daoist sage in the *Zhuangzi*.

Let me quote another story from the *Zhuangzi*. It is, again, about the shrewd outlaw of ancient China, the robber Zhi. I once again make a contemporary comparison to highlight the moral outrage that was associated with his name in ancient China. The robber Zhi was a sort of Osama bin Laden. He was the head of a criminal organization that terrorized the country and was infamous for all sorts of crimes and cruelties. In the *Zhuangzi* the following exchange occurs between this outlaw and one of his followers—written in a style similar to the famous short dialogues between Confucius and his disciples. It goes as follows:

> So when one of Robber Zhi's band asked him: "Do robbers too have the Way?" Zhi answered: "A shrewd guess at where the things are hidden in the house is the Intuitiveness of the sage. Being first man in is Courage. Being the last man out is Duty. Knowing whether or not you can bring it off is Wisdom. Giving everyone fair shares is Goodwill. Without these five at his disposal, no one in the world could ever make a great robber."[10]

Thugs and terrorists are not without morality—or, in ancient Chinese terminology, "the way" (*dao*). They normally believe themselves to be more moral than their victims. Osama bin Laden believes that he is fighting for a just cause. The same belief is shared by his followers. They claim to act in the name of the very same moral values for which others condemn them. Morality is not in the act itself; it is an aspect of the language or the semantics with which the act is evaluated—on both sides. Morality is much more a tool of interpretation or social struggle than something that is unequivocally tied to certain events. It is always up for grabs.

Morality is not so much an inner conviction that prevents people from doing bad things as a rhetorical device that helps them justify their actions before and after they act. In fact morality often leads people to commit extreme acts in the name of good—that others will view as bad or even evil. The *Zhuangzi* observes that *this* is the primary effect of morality. A society in which there is a lot of moral talk will not have fewer crimes. All the moralists in the world have not, so far, prevented war and murder. There is no correlation between more moral talk and a better world. Moral language, in fact, seems to be part of the problem, not the solution. This is why the *Zhuangzi* comments on the dialogue between the robber Zhi and his follower:

> Judging by this, without the Way of the sage the good man would not stand, without the Way of the sage Robber Zhi would not walk. If the good men in the world are fewer than the bad, the sages have

benefited the world less than they have harmed it. With the birth of the sages the great robbers arise. Smash the sages, turn the thieves and bandits loose, and for the first time the world will be in order. . . . Once the sages are dead the great robbers will not arise, the world will be at peace and there will be no more trouble.[11]

According to the *Zhuangzi*, what we need to make the world a safer and more peaceful place is not more morality, but less. Peace and morality are not the same. In fact, they are quite often opposed to one another.

I conclude my reflections on the negative ethics of the *Zhuangzi* with a discussion of another of its philosophically relevant features, namely its nonhumanism. In accordance with the thesis that there is no need for morality in a nonpathological social state, the *Zhuangzi* explains: "In an age when Power [*de*] is at its utmost, they don't 'promote excellence,' don't 'employ ability.' The man above is like a treetop; the people are like wild deer. They are upright but do not know how to think of it as Duty [*yi*], love each other but do not know how to think of it as Goodwill [*ren*], are genuine but do not think of it as Loyalty [*zhong*], keep their word but do not know how to think of it as Good Faith [*xin*]."[12] In an amoral society both the ruler and the ruled lose their human characteristics: they are like the treetop and the wild deer. This is perhaps the most radical claim of the *Zhuangzi*'s negative ethics. It runs counter to the dominant Confucian morality of ancient China—and here the emphasis is not only on the specific moral values advocated by the Confucians but also on their general project of human cultivation. Confucian humanism is flatly opposed, the ideal social state is one in which the animal nature flourishes.

The antimoralism of the *Zhuangzi*'s negative ethics is an important component of its nonhumanist and decidedly nonanthropocentric approach. Early Daoist philosophy, I believe, attempts to create conceptions of society, the cosmos, and the individual that do not focus primarily on human qualities. I cannot discuss this issue here in detail,[13] but I believe that such an interpretation makes it adaptable to the posthumanist voices in our contemporary philosophical discourse.[14] Such voices have increased in intensity, and there is at least one, the English author John Gray, who draws heavily on Daoist sources. I conclude this chapter with a brief discussion of his treatise in *Straw Dogs: Thoughts on Humans and Other Animals* that includes a contemporary version of a posthumanist and anti-moralist negative ethics.

For Gray, modern Western humanism is the secular successor of Christian theology. Humans are the only beings that can exercise free will and are consequently responsible for improving this world. According to Gray, nineteenth-century thinkers such as the French positivists (Saint-Simon, Comte), the English liberals (Mill), and Karl Marx secularized the belief in human agency. Their brand of humanism is "the post-Christian faith that humans can make a world better than any in which they have so far lived"; it "is the transformation of this Christian doctrine of salvation into a project of universal human emancipation."[15]

According to Gray, the modern Western narratives of progress, of the human mastery of the world, and of the omnipotence of science and rationality, are not much more than illusions of control and power. From his antihumanist perspective, humans are a product of blind evolutionary drift and this world is not primarily man's world. Instead of an anthropocentric worldview, Gray subscribes to the Gaia hypothesis, that is, "the theory that the Earth is a self-regulating sys-tem whose behaviour resembles in some ways that of an organism."[16] In the light of this hypothesis, ascriptions of conscious control and free choice are mere human vanities. The larger systems within which humans exist are not and cannot be steered by humans. They are rather to be conceived of as self-steering and self-reproducing.

One of the main by-products of the humanist narrative of mas-tery is the belief in moral normativity. Modern Western moral phi-losophy can be conceived of as a secularization of Christian values: "We inherit our belief—or pretence—that moral values take prece-dence over all other valuable things from a variety of sources, but chiefly from Christianity."[17] Moral philosophies are an integral part of the narratives of rational control and social progress that were developed during and after the Enlightenment. In practice, however, the projects of moral progress often led to disaster. One may think of Robespierre's worship of virtue during the Terror in 1794, and, in particular, of the much more extensive and destructive experiments of more recent times in Russia, Germany, and China. Gray states:

"What makes the twentieth century special is not the fact that it is littered with massacres. It is the scale of its killings and the fact that they were premeditated for the sake of vast projects of world improvement. Progress and mass murder run in tandem."[18]

As an alternative to the humanist moral projects of modernity, Gray advocates a Daoist approach and praises "animal virtues," that is, the virtues that come naturally and without effort. Virtue, in his view, does not consist in the establishment of rational duties and moral norms, but in acting spontaneously. Whereas morality is, for him, "a sickness peculiar to humans, the good life is a refinement of the virtues of animals. Arising from our animal natures, ethics needs no ground."[19] He sums up his posthumanist, new Daoist version of negative ethics in the following passage:

> The fact that we are not autonomous subjects deals a death blow to morality—but it is the only possible ground of ethics. . . . In everyday life we do not scan our options beforehand, then enact the one that is best. We simply deal with whatever is at hand. We get up in the morning and put on our clothes without meaning to do so. We help a friend in the same way. . . . Outside the Western tradition, the Daoists of ancient China saw no gap between is and ought. Right action was whatever comes from a clear view of the situation. They did not follow moralists—in their day, Confucians—in wanting to fetter human beings with rules or principles. For Daoists, the good life is only the natural life lived skillfully. It has no practical purpose. It has nothing to do with the will, and it does not consist in trying to realize any ideal.[20]

This is, in my view, as close as one can get to the negative ethics of the Daoist moral fool in contemporary theory.

21

A PATHOLOGY OF ETHICS

A PATHOLOGY OF ETHICS

3 | THE REDUNDANCY OF ETHICS

AT THE END of the preceding chapter, I quoted John Gray saying that in everyday life we usually do not think or act morally. We put our clothes on in the morning without any ethical purpose in mind, and continue like this throughout much of the day. Only in extraordinary situations are we forced—or feel forced, or force ourselves—to think and act morally. The same is said, more poetically I believe, in the following passage from the *Zhuangzi*: "If you step on someone's foot in the market you make a formal apology for your carelessness; an elder brother says he hopes it didn't hurt; father and mother are too close kin to say anything at all."[1] The closer and more familiar you are the less need there is for artificial politeness—a simple smile will do. Stepping on somebody else's foot only becomes an ethical issue if you are not closely related. An ethical stance and ethical communication typically go along with a potential for conflict. Once your step is potentially deemed unethical, you need to make apologies to prevent discord. The need for virtues and ethical behavior arises from a lack of natural harmony. They are more indicative of a social problem than of a harmonious situation. As Niklas Luhmann puts it: "In normal everyday interaction, after all, morality is not needed anyway; it is always a symptom of the occurrence of pathologies."[2]

In this chapter I argue that, on the one hand, morality is not called for in most of our activities. In fact it is typically made use of in what can be called a social crisis. Just as the moral distinction between good and evil is an extreme form of distinguishing between good and bad, the need for morality typically arises in extreme situations. On the other hand, I suggest that in many social contexts morality does more harm than good. It is therefore often completely redundant and, in some cases, even a nuisance.

I discuss three examples of circumstances in everyday life in which morality is redundant. The first one is addressed in the introduction. In the relation between parents and children, morality normally plays only a secondary role. I mention the case of a baby who cries all night. Nobody would expect the parents to be morally outraged because of this, although most would admit to being frustrated and annoyed. It is natural for parents to love their children. And this prevents them from bringing moral categories into play. The same is true for most parental criticism and in the not infrequent quarrels between parents and children. If parents scold a child, they normally do not view the child as evil—even if there was some serious mischief. This does not mean that the parents approve of what the child did, but they do not morally condemn her. If they did so, this would indicate a serious disturbance of the normal parent-child relationship. Mutual love would be in jeopardy. If one introduces ethical reasoning into family affairs, there is a high potential for conflict and discord, and, again, not of simple disagreement or dispute but of some rather extreme tension. Love within the family makes morality obsolete. Parents and children are, in most cultures, not expected to mutually condemn each other ethically. Parents are, on the contrary, expected to love their children despite potential moral shortcomings. And this holds true the other way around as well.

It has, of course, to be admitted that parents normally try to educate their children morally. But this, paradoxically, does not mean that they apply morality while they teach moral judgments. If a brother beats his sister, then most parents will admonish the boy. But, in the end, they will hopefully not love the son less than the daughter. Recourse to ethics will occur in more or less extreme situations (as when siblings fight), but it will not trump the more essential emotional ties between family members. If parents judge their children primarily in moral terms, significant emotional harm is likely.

There are instances in which such a conflict between morality and family love occurs. Typical cases are of a sexual nature. In many cultures, for instance, premarital sex is looked upon as highly immoral, even inexcusable. If this happens, it is sometimes morally expected that the parents will expel or even kill their daughter. I cannot imagine that such a moral imposition on a family would not cause extraordinary emotional and social suffering. It may be argued that such an example shows that a wrong or immoral morality (having to kill your daughter for having premarital sex) causes harm— but what about cases in our society in which parents are supposed to morally condemn their children, or wives their husbands? Is the situation different in the case of a sexual behavior, such as child pornography, that we deem highly immoral? Would not a similar conflict between moral expectations and intimate emotions arise? The point that I am trying to make is this: Within a family, morality does not rule—nor should it. Love within the family is, normally, not correlated with moral judgments. It is only in extreme cases that morality rules—and when it rules it is a symptom of the breakdown of harmonious family relations.

A second example of the redundancy of morality is sports—but what I say about sports could be extended to many other activities that are guided by certain rules and in which the rules are more or less strictly enforced. Educational institutions, schools and universities for instance, function on the basis of rules. Most competitive sports presuppose a relatively strict set of rules—U.S. football is a prime example. These rules are necessary for a number of reasons. First of all, they grant more or less equal advantages and disadvantages to the competitors so that the result of the game cannot be predicted. Second, there have to be rules in order to provide structure to the game. Without rules it would be very hard to identify the game in the first place. In sports that involve a lot of body contact, rules are necessary to ensure the safety of the participants. They are also required so that the distinction between the winners and the losers can be made. None of these functions are moral. Professional wrestling, a parody of sport, illustrates these points. Unlike in a real sports competition, there are no explicit rules in place; the result is fixed; and the safety of the combatants is made a mockery of—and there is more often than not a moral storyline or narrative attached to the show. Professional wrestling is a comedy that demonstrates what would happen to sport if it were a moral activity.

An important nonmoral aspect of the rules in sports is that they apply only within and for the duration of the game. If someone violates a rule, he or she gets a penalty or, in the worst case, is expelled from the game. This does not, however, normally result in a moral judgment that transcends the boundaries of the game and applies to the character of the participant. Only in an extreme case will a rule breaker be deemed bad or evil. In fact, sportsmanship consists partly in being able to shake hands after the game and leave without holding a grudge. Winning and losing are supposed to be entirely free of morality. It is seen as a violation of the code of sports if losers are blamed for their loss other than on the basis of criteria related to their athletic performance. If a coach blames his players morally, this signals an acute problem. Sometimes, of course, players are morally criticized. This can happen if they were not fully committed to the game, or more seriously, they used performance-enhancing drugs or physically attacked a rival. But these are indicators of an exceptional situation, of a crisis. They signal the end of sports, and such cases are usually pursued by means that transcend the actual competition. A player may be fired, that is, economically sanctioned, or brought before the legal system.

During the game, moral judgments are supposed to stay outside the arena. Nobody is supposed to view the competition in moral terms. If moral categories enter the game, it is immediately endangered. It is very difficult to proceed normally if the opponents consider each other evil, and violence can easily erupt if a team's supporters hold that view. To prevent this there are all sorts of ceremonial gestures before, during, and after the game (I mentioned shaking hands, but there are also other conventions) that demonstrate its nonmoral character.

Fairness in sports is not an ethical issue, but an issue of following rules and conventions. Those who act unfairly get sanctioned—but not morally, except in unusual cases. The same applies to the worship of sports heroes. Although a star may be praised for his outstanding personality off the field, this is only a minor and often somewhat staged embellishment of his athletic achievements. Legends in sports, such as Babe Ruth, Wayne Gretzky, and Pelé, are not primarily moral champions. One of the functions of sport is, perhaps, that it gives us a break from moral judgments. It allows us to play with the good/bad distinction in an unserious manner. We know that even if our team loses, this does not result in a moral evaluation.

In many activities and relationships we do not make use of moral categories and are—not in spite of, but because of this—able to get along perfectly well with others. In most normal situations there is no need for being either moral or immoral; we can simply be amoral. To further elaborate on this point, I present a third example that was suggested by my colleague Franklin Perkins: deciding whether to cheat on one's romantic partner. I think that even in this situation one can be a moral fool and, moreover, that most people would probably act as such. There are three possible ethical positions by which one can approach this dilemma: the immoral, the moral, and the amoral. An immoral person would simply ignore all moral considerations and deliberately violate every given moral principle. The moral person, on the contrary, would base her decision solely on ethical convictions (as, for instance, formulated by religion, social environment, or ideology). The amoral person would not rely on ethical principles but do whatever she does with mixed feelings. There will be no simple solution dictated by a definite moral rule. She would never know if what she was doing (in either case) was absolutely justified. I think the amoral position is actually the most considerate of the three since considerations do not end with a given ethical norm but will include emotions (whom do I really love more?), practical deliberations (which relationship is more feasible?), and personal constraints (how will my children react?)—none of which are of a primarily ethical nature. I also think that the amoral position is the most realistic one because most people would probably not rely only on ethical standards (or deliberately act in opposition to them). After the fact, many would say to themselves: I did what I did because it was ethical. But is this really true? They most likely did it because they thought it was a good thing to do—but good and ethical are not necessarily the same.

The first two examples discussed above illustrate the two most important antidotes of morality: love, when it comes to intimate relationships, and law, when it comes to nonintimate social relations.[3] Love and law are social mechanisms that lead to the suspension and obsolescence of morality. They will, in most cases, not entirely extinguish morality, but keep it in check. As antidotes, love and the law are able to prevent morality from inflaming the social body. With respect to morality, penal law is intended to function similarly to rules and regulations in sports. A penalty will suspend a player for some time from participating in the game or apply some other form of sanction. It is understood, however, that the player should not suffer any consequences beyond those immediately related to the game. A total rehabilitation is intended. A player may even be suspended for several games, but this is not meant to have an effect on her personally or result in some sort of discrimination when she returns to the game. Penal law is also meant, in most cases, to provide for the possibility of total rehabilitation. Once the time is done or the fine is paid, one is supposed to be allowed to go on with one's life more or less unimpeded.

Unlike legal punishment, moral judgments do not come with an expiration date. The antidote for sin—forgiveness—can only be administered by (God's) love. If not for love or the law, moral condemnations would tend to continue. The law, of course, can also punish—in extreme cases—in an unlimited way. Many countries still practice the death penalty—but I argue in chapter 11 that this is an indicator of moral contamination of the law and therefore a highly problematic legal measure to begin with. Some offenders are given life sentences or are confined to medical institutions. This is mostly justified, however, on pragmatic grounds. To set such a dangerous offender free is seen as highly risky. A sexual predator is confined not primarily for moral reasons but to protect others (and, one could argue, even himself) from further harm. Love and the law are social mechanisms that, in my view, are effective substitutes for morality. They allow society to deal with (extreme) cases of norm violations in a coherent and practical manner. They allow for the rehabilitation and reintegration of offenders by limiting sanctions and offering the potential for reconciliation, the reestablishment of harmony, and the resolution of conflicts.

The third example introduced above deals with a common problem in life. One often has to make a decision that cannot be dealt with by legal means and where love does not provide a solution. It may therefore be argued that morality is not at all redundant in everyday life, that there are many cases in which one has to make a moral choice. I think the cheating spouse example demonstrates that, first, even in normal life, the (presumed) need for moral choices is rather limited. Most situations in your daily life—having breakfast, driving to work, doing your job, watching TV at night—do not confront you with moral dilemmas. Most people find themselves rather infrequently in a situation where they have to decide whether to cheat on their partner.

Though moral dilemmas are the exception rather than the rule, they nonetheless occur. Moralists may say that such exceptions are the defining moments in life, that they are the most crucial and critical events. I think that such a defining situation is usually not dealt with by morality alone, and not even primarily by recourse to moral criteria. Critical situations tend to be very complex. This is what makes them critical. They are problematic because they are extraordinary and thus there is no simple way of dealing with them. A number of factors come into play and these factors conflict with one another. It is difficult to make a decision because so many things have to be taken into account and there are no clear priorities to be discerned. In such situations moral considerations may be helpful and contribute to one's decision, but the decision may become highly problematic if these moral considerations trump all others. Someone who decides on moral principles alone, a moral fundamentalist, may well end up with an impractical decision, a decision that hurts those he is close to and perhaps even violates the law.

A story that illustrates this very well is Heinrich von Kleist's *Michael Kohlhaas*. Michael Kohlhaas is the opposite of the moral fool. He is a highly moral man who suffers an obvious injustice. This infuriates him, and he ventures on a crusade that soon becomes a major social upheaval. In a way, he turns into the criminal leader of a marauding mob and ruins not only his own life but also those of his family and followers. There is no doubt, at least in the beginning, that Michael Kohlhaas was morally right, but the result of founding his actions on moral considerations was disastrous. Here a relatively minor injustice initiated a severe social crisis that resulted in significant harm. The story shows that what is morally right is not necessarily good. In fact, decisions based solely on a feeling of what is morally right may lead to, in Hegel's terms, a "frenzy of self-conceit."[4]

Even if one agrees that morality is often redundant, it could still be argued that, nevertheless, it is essential to define the *values* of society. One could say that moral values—such as justice, equality, freedom, and caring—are the foundation of family life, the legal system, and everyday interaction, and thus of society as a whole. One could say that what I have called one of the antidotes against morality, namely love, is in fact a moral value and the ethical cornerstone of Christianity.

My view of love, however, is more Confucian than Christian. Confucians view love in terms of affection as the natural emotional bond within a family—and not as a virtue or a moral value. I do not agree with the Christian vision of universal love, and I do not think that there can or should be an ethical obligation to love others. While it is a serious problem when family members do not love one another, an appeal to ethical values cannot create the love that is lacking. One can be encouraged to support, care for, or respect family members, but it is impossible to love someone you do not. Not loving a child is not immoral but sad. Perhaps a realization of duty, and thus, in the Kantian sense, a moral insight, could replace love in the family. Parents who don't love their children may still regard it as their duty to care for and respect them. But I would suggest that substituting morality for love in such circumstances is not more effective or better than, for instance, a juridical order to pay child support.

Turning to the law, clearly, in contemporary society legal decisions are typically not based on the evaluation of moral values but on legal evaluation. Consider, for example, the moral debate that surrounds abortion. One side argues that there is the absolute moral (or religious or both) duty to protect life. On the other side, people argue that there is an ethical obligation to respect a women's control over her body. In most liberal societies, however, legislation on abortion is not based on which of these two positions is morally superior. Judges do not decide if a woman is morally justified in having an abortion, but if she is legally justified in doing so. That a woman has the legal right to an abortion does not mean that she has—or does not have—the moral right to do so. A legal decision on abortion does not solve moral questions. Moral values have an extrajuridical dimension that the law should not take into account. A legal decision is not meant to judge moral values but to interpret and perhaps modify existing law. That is, decisions are made on the basis of legal coherence and not on ethics.[5] A judge or jury is supposed to be concerned with what is in line with existing law, not with what is in line with certain values.

In our society a legal system that functions well is "operationally closed"—to use Niklas Luhmann's terminology. This means that it is distinct from moral, religious, political, and economic communication. Juridical decisions are not supposed to be moral, religious, political, or economic. This does not mean that such concerns do not influence the legal system, but that this influence does not disrupt its autonomy. A legal system, if it functions well, is able to withstand outside pressure and come up with decisions that are, in the end, neither moral, religious, political, or economic, but simply legal. Legal values, that is, rights, may well be *derived* from moral, religious, political, and economic values, but the decisive fact is that rights had to decouple themselves from these values to become legal rights. There is, both in the synchronic and diachronic dimension, a social environment for the legal system that includes such values (life, liberty, property, etc.), but within the legal system those values become rights, and thus their function is very different from moral or religious values.

A society in which the law is dominated by moral, religious, or political values is a society without an autonomous legal system. There are countries in which political ideologies, religions, or a certain economic stratum totally controls the legal system. If, for instance, religion dominates the legal system, then the religious authorities can easily ban abortion. This has happened in several countries. Under these circumstances one set of values overpowers all others. The problem with moral values is that they often conflict with each other—as is the case with respect to abortion. In a religious society, there will be a definite decision on such issues on the basis of a specific hierarchy of moral or religious values. Here morality, religion, and the law all run in parallel. In a functionally differentiated society, however, there is not a fixed set of values, and moral, religious, legal, political, and economic values are not in line. Again, in most modern societies, a legal right does not automatically translate into a specific moral or religious right—and vice versa. A society in which these values do not converge, is, in my view, preferable to a society in which they do. Even if legal rights are derived from or influenced by moral (and other) values, it is, I think, the place of the legal system to come up with its own amoral (and areligious etc.) values. This makes moral values, to a certain degree, redundant.

We do not spend much of our time reflecting on foundational moral values as we go about our daily lives. Most of our decisions are arrived at amorally. Even in critical situations we consider relevant nonmoral values. If, however, we make a decision based only on moral values, we still have to choose between the "stars in the sky."[6] There is no intrinsic or official hierarchy of moral values. Moral values do not provide some sort of foolproof guidance in everyday life. There is no common agreement on which values are the most valuable, and after you take action, others can always accuse you of having made an *immoral* decision. Moral criteria may be influential in deciding certain issues, but it cannot be said that such values provide a firm foundation for everyday interaction in society. Empirically speaking, moral values simply do not provide ultimate guidance. There are no moral values that supply one with concrete guidance for how to act in specific situations. One can justify one's actions—for instance, with respect to abortion—with reference to moral values, but one cannot derive a factual ethical solution to such a problem. It can be determined if an abortion is factually legal or illegal, but it cannot be determined if it is factually moral or immoral. We may believe that it is moral or immoral—but we will never, and can never, know.

4 | THE "MORALITY OF ANGER"

ONE OF THE FEELINGS I find most uncomfortable, so uncomfortable that I lose sleep, is what is called righteous anger. If I have suffered from what I see as a grave injustice that remains unpunished I find it hard to regain my equilibrium. It is not only that I have suffered an injustice, but more importantly that this injustice has not been recognized as such—I have been treated meanly and it has gone publicly unnoticed. Perhaps I was, for the moment, unable to find the right reply to an insult, or maybe I was right when others thought me wrong. Such situations can cause great emotional suffering and generate this righteous anger. The plots of innumerable novels, movies, and plays revolve around similar conflicts. Typically, the catharsis is reached only at the very end as the moral balance is reconstituted when the evil receive their punishment and the good, against all odds, finally prevail. Righteous anger subsides only when the moral crisis is solved.

In real life, however, I have noticed that the moral crises often remain unresolved. I may have an unbelievably hypocritical colleague at work who, on a daily basis, violates the most basic rules of decency but always gets away with it. I may have a greedy family member who treats her closest relatives shamefully but there is nothing that can be legally done about this. I may know a person who is selfish and has no shame, but has a splendid career and gets richer each year. When I think about these people I find it hard to repress my anger and not to yearn for retribution and justice. But such yearnings are seldom fulfilled.

Anger and morality can be very closely connected. It is easy to be angry with someone we conceive of as evil. Unfortunately, though, this emotion typically harms those who feel it much more than those about whom it is felt.

It seems that there are only two ways to dispel righteous anger. Either the evil person is finally brought to justice or one ceases to conceive of the evildoer in moral terms. Either revenge is meted out or one manages to simply forget about the perceived wrong. The problem with the first solution is that it is more likely, and easier to find, in fiction than in reality. The problem with the second is that it is very hard to forget what is felt so strongly. These two ways can also be labeled the moral and the amoral solutions to—or, perhaps better, dissolution of—anger.

A strong proponent of the first solution is the U.S. author Walter Berns, who passionately advocates the death penalty on the basis of a "morality of anger."[1] I discuss the specific connection between morality and the death penalty that is outlined by Berns later in this book and focus here only on the psychological aspects of his theory. His argument is very straightforward. He believes that "anger is somehow connected with justice" and explains: "If men [sic] are not angry when a neighbor suffers at the hand of a criminal, the implication is that their moral faculties have been corrupted, that they are not good citizens." Or more generally: "A moral community is not possible without anger and the moral indignation that accompanies it."[2]

Anger and morality are, from this perspective, mutually supportive. They are good and necessary both for individuals and for the community. Anger (about evildoers) is a reaction to the violation of moral norms and thus a righteous and noble (even if painful) feeling. Morality leads to anger, and anger leads to morality, or as Berns claims, the lack of anger indicates a lack of morality (which could be a reason for further anger). Punishing the evildoer is thus an emotional and a moral necessity. It relieves the person who was righteously angry and restores the moral equilibrium by "paying back" the offender.[3] According to Berns, a morality of anger is both individually and socially healthy. The moral and mental health of individuals and societies can be measured by the righteous anger they are able to produce.

Berns rightly refers to Aristotle in his discussion of the relation between anger and morality.[4] Still, at least to my mind, Aristotle's version of a morality of anger is subtler than Berns' and much less polemic. In his treatise on rhetoric, Aristotle presents—among many other intricate examinations of emotions, feelings, and their relevance in successful argumentation and persuasion—a sort of case study on anger [*orgē*] and how to make use of it in public speech. Aristotle outlines a peculiar dialectics of anger and begins his analysis with the following definition: "Let anger be [defined as] desire accompanied by [mental and physical] distress, for conspicuous retaliation, because of a conspicuous slight that was directed, without justification, against oneself or those near to one."[5] This understanding of anger and morality is very similar to Berns'. Anger is the result of (moral) injustice. As long as there has been no retaliation for that injustice one feels anger, and this feeling is distressing or painful. Aristotle is quick to add, however, that "a kind of pleasure follows all experience of anger from the hope of getting retaliation." And he illustrates this with a quote from the *Iliad*: "A thing much sweeter than honey in the throat, it grows in the breasts of men." The feeling of anger is highly ambiguous. On the one hand, we are harmed by it, but on the other hand, it leads us to fantasies of revenge that can be quite stimulating. Aristotle explains: "A kind of pleasure follows from this and also because people dwell in their minds on retaliating; then the image [*phantasia*] that occurs creates pleasure, as in the case of dreams."[6] This particular tension between pain and pleasure is, according to Aristotle, the psychological core of the feeling of anger. It is also what makes the literary and cinematic works that deal with revenge so attractive. Anger is an ambiguous experience. The suffering associated with it is coupled with the promise of gratification. Berns' morality of anger obviously embraces this—which makes his ethics one of impulse. It is based on the craving for revenge and its emotional dialectics of pain and pleasure. The morality of anger is the outcome of a specific human "desire"—to quote Aristotle again. This is a morality based not on norms, principles, or rules of behavior but on sentiment.

In the *Rhetoric*, Aristotle looks in detail at the specific sources of moral anger and pays particular attention to being slighted. In a society like ancient Greece, where ethics were mainly based on manners and public behavior, slights and insults were regarded very seriously. When honor is the foundation of social prestige, an insult is a public degradation and it calls for a response. Aristotle's analysis of the slight is therefore culturally specific and does not apply seamlessly to contemporary circumstances. This is not to say that insults do not still provoke anger, but today other indecencies (as in the three hypothetical cases outlined at the beginning of chapter 3) may be seen as equally offensive or even more so. The culturally specific focus in Aristotle's morality of anger, however, does not take anything away from the more general insight into the emotional dialectics of anger that goes along with it. Interestingly enough, Aristotle contrasts moral anger with *calmness*. He states: "Let calmness be [defined as] a settling down and quieting of anger."[7] Calmness is thus defined as the relief from or the dissolution of anger.

The most important aspect of Aristotle's theory is, however, an aspect that is neglected in Berns' ethical argumentation. Aristotle writes on the morality of anger and calmness in his book on rhetoric. This is to say, his ultimate intention is neither ethical nor psychological, but rhetorical. He deals with morality and moral sentiments for the sake of explaining how an effective speech can be created. He is concerned with the practical consequences of his theory, that is to say, with *applied* moral psychology. He is very clear about this when he introduces his analysis of calmness: "Since becoming calm is the opposite of becoming angry, and anger the opposite of calmness [*praotēs*], the state of mind of those who are calm should be grasped [by a speaker] and toward whom they are calm and for what reasons." Similarly, he concludes his analysis of anger by saying that "it is clear that it might be needful in speech to put [the audience] in the state of mind of those who are inclined to anger and to show one's opponents as responsible for those things that are the causes of anger and that they are the sort of people against whom anger is directed."[8]

Aristotle is very explicit that his moral psychology is supposed to be used as a *rhetorical tool*. The skillful orator is able to arouse moral sentiments in his (in the ancient Greek context) audience and these are angry sentiments. If you want to stir up the public then one of the most effective—if not the single most effective—tools is to let your audience feel righteous anger. The orator's task is to transform a calm audience into an angry audience. And moral speech is perhaps the most effective way to achieve this. The morality of anger that Berns talks about is not so much an ethical principle, but a social, or more specifically, rhetorical, semantic, or communications tool. Following Aristotle, the morality of anger is a social skill; following Berns, it is an indicator of individual and social health. But if, as Berns, suggests, anger indeed indicates mental and social health, then we can infer, with Aristotle, that such health consists in transforming calm individuals and calm communities into angry ones. Agreement among philosophers on this use of anger is not unanimous. There are some who believe that calmness is both preferable and healthier.

The Daoists were not the only Eastern philosophers who were suspicious of states of excitement, especially moral excitement. The most prominent of these are probably the Buddhists. I concentrate here on Zen (or, in Chinese, Chan) Buddhism. Unlike Daoism, Buddhism is very much concerned with the problem of suffering and so subscribes to what may be called the soteriological project of dissolving it. Zen is, obviously, only one branch of Buddhism and there are a wide variety of schools and approaches that I have to ignore here. In the tradition of Yogācāra Buddhism, Zen Buddhism looked upon suffering as primarily a mental issue Its practices were aimed at cultivating a state of mind that would be free from suffering. This state can, in the Buddhist terminology, be called enlightenment, but one should not confuse this with any kind of transcendent elevation of consciousness. Like Daoism, Zen Buddhism is based on a thoroughly immanent worldview that does not aim at anything "beyond." With respect to morality this means that the negative ethics of Zen Buddhism does not intend (unlike Kierkegaard) to replace a moral outlook with a transcendent religious one that operates on a higher plane. The Zen Buddhists, like the Daoists, were more interested in resolving problems here and now.

I think that the Zen Buddhist approach to morality can quite well be explained as the counterproject to what is described in Aristotle's *Rhetoric*. Aristotle advises the prospective orator on how to incite wrath in his audience. The section on the morality of anger provides guidance on how to transform calmness into moral anger and shows how this emotional state is a complex combination of pain and pleasure. The Zen Buddhists would, I presume, agree with Aristotle's psychological analysis. They would admit that moral consciousness goes along with passionate feelings of pain and pleasure. Unlike Aristotle (and, in particular, unlike Walter Berns), however, they do not agree that such a state is desirable. Instead, because anger is so intricately connected with emotional pain, they seek to neutralize it. If suffering is to end, then states of consciousness that evoke pain have to be extinguished. They therefore advocate strategies for the dissolution of moral feelings in order to transform (moral) anger into calmness.[9]

Unlike Aristotle in the *Rhetoric*, the Zen Buddhists do not focus on rhetorical means to alter emotional states and social behavior. In fact, they are not so concerned with altering the feelings and actions of others as they are with altering their own. They are more interested in silent meditation than in eloquent persuasion. Zen Buddhist meditation aims at calming the mind, and in order to do this, one has to address one's own moral sentiments and anger.

"Do not think good, do not think evil" is advice given to the Zen Buddhist practioner.[10] A variation of this phrase is found in Dazhu Huihai's (late eighth/early ninth century CE) *Dunwu rudao yaomen lun*: "Thinking in terms of good and evil is wrong; not to think so is right thinking. The same applies to all the other categories of opposites—sorrow and joy, beginning and end, acceptance and rejection, dislikes and likes, aversion and love, all of which are called wrong thinking, while to abstain from thinking in those categories is called right thinking."[11] "Thinking" here refers to the activity of the mind during meditation—and, by extension, of the enlightened person who no longer suffers. This state of mind is not so different from that of the moral fool in Daoism. One simply refrains from attaching substantial value judgments to one's perceptions, and a prime value judgment is obviously moral judgment. That such thinking is wrong does not mean that what is good is not good and that what is bad is not bad, but to think in these terms leads to mental distress. It is wrong not with respect to its veracity, but wrong if one hopes to dissolve suffering. Right thinking is not thinking that is correct in the sense of corresponding to the facts, but in the sense that it leads to calmness. From the Zen Buddhist perspective moral judgments are among the most disturbing judgments since they easily lead to such feelings as anger. An angry state of mind is not only painful—and thus wrong—it also obscures one's vision or, perhaps, overshadows it. What is perceived angrily is not perceived rightly.

It is important to note that for the Zen Buddhists, as well as for the Daoists, emotional indifference is not to be equated with a simple attitude of "all is one." The opposite is the case: The superimposition of an emotional coloring on perception blurs perception. Passionate love, as the proverb more or less says, makes one blind. Huihai therefore says: "In the midst of all such pairs of opposites as good and evil, you are able to distinguish between them without being stained by them and, in this way, to reach the state of being perfectly at ease and free of all dependence." And, even more clearly: "Ability to distinguish the minutest differences among the appearances constituting our environment, as well as the smallest gradations of good and evil, and yet to be so entirely unaffected by them that we remain perfectly at ease amidst all of them—that is called the Wisdom Vision."[12]

The indifferent and amoral mind sees more clearly than the emotionally and morally afflicted one. This enlightened perspective that the Zen Buddhists aspire to acquire is perhaps not so different from that of a good judge. A good judge is able to clearly see what is right and wrong (in a legal sense) without having her vision blurred by moral judgments. If a judge feels moral anger toward a defendant, she will not be able to treat him "fairly," in the sense of juridical impartiality. That a judge avoids moral judgments does not diminish but rather enhances her ability to come to an appropriate legal judgment. A judge is not supposed to found her judgment on her moral beliefs or sentiments. And if the judge remains morally detached from her cases, she will probably also be able to cope better with them psychologically. A judge who became morally involved in all her cases would likely develop serious mental health problems. Zen Buddhists are not concerned with legal impartiality but with more encompassing and general impartiality. The effect of this impartiality is, however, comparable to the effect that moral impartiality can have for a judge; both of them allow a situation to be viewed impartially and with less emotional suffering.

The Zen Buddhist position is nicely summarized by Huihai: "The ten evils are killing, stealing, licentiousness, lying, voluptuous speech, slander, coarse language, covetousness, anger and false views. The ten virtues may be simply defined as absence of the ten evils." It is quite clear that this position has gone a step further than conventional Buddhist ethics. The amoral position of Zen does not deny that such deeds as killing and stealing—and anger—are socially harmful and thus wrong, but it avoids contrasting this catalog with a catalog of virtues since this would result in a dualist moral mindset. The translator John Blofeld rightfully remarks on this passage: "This negative approach to the ten virtues indicates that, when the higher stages of the path are reached, clinging to virtue as something positive is as much an obstacle as clinging to evil."[13] Such a negative ethics seeks to avoid the trappings of a morality of anger that thinks in terms of vices and virtues. If one looks at socially unacceptable and harmful actions in moral terms, calmness will be replaced by anger. Becoming angry prevents one from becoming enlightened, and, paradoxically, is simply one more wrong. Huihai seems to imply that by reacting with moral anger to what is obviously wrong, one creates another wrong.

The Zen Buddhists were quite radical in going beyond conventional Buddhist ethics that, in other schools, could be quite moralistic and include all sorts of concrete prescriptions and proscriptions. One of the most radical and outspoken of the famous Zen masters was Linji (d. 866). His recorded sayings include the following passage—which itself is somewhat angry, but, as I would argue, playfully or ironically or paradoxically so: "There's a bunch of fellows who can't tell good from bad but poke around in the scriptural teachings, hazard a guess here and there, and come up with an idea in words, as though they took a lump of shit, mushed it around in their mouth, and then spat it out and passed it on to somebody else."[14]

Linji makes fun of the Buddhist moralists and is not shy in his choice of words. The moralists do not have an adequate view of life and rely only on moral guidelines that they have sheepishly taken from the scriptures. They are pious men and women but by following the doctrines and knowing exactly how to tell right from wrong they actually lose the capability of right thinking in the sense of Huihai. The moral doctrines that can be found in the Buddhist classics are, in Linji's view, worthless and hollow. To simply propagate them is nothing more than a rhetorical exercise. Rather than actually bringing about individual and social calmness (or enlightenment), they result in establishing moralist attitudes that lead to a morality of anger that, from a Zen Buddhist perspective, is quite unhealthy. The Buddhist moralists, in Linji's view, pass ethical shit around and pollute society.

Zen Buddhists like Linji did not claim to be holy men and did not try to convert anyone. They did not advocate a religious lifestyle in the sense of clinging to some specific doctrine or practice. For them, the problem with traditional Buddhism was that it had developed into a formal teaching and institutionalized routine that was no longer helpful in reducing suffering. They certainly saw themselves as pursuing the type of the enlightenment that the Buddha himself had presumably achieved, but they did not think that it consisted in acquiring a certain set of fixed beliefs or getting to a higher state of consciousness. Linji stated—and one finds many similar passages in the records of other Zen masters: "I tell you, there's no Buddha, no Dharma, no practice, no enlightenment. Yet you go off like this on side roads, trying to find something. Blind fools! Will you put another head on top of the one you have? What is it you lack?" And he added: "The way I see it, there's no call for anything special. Just act ordinary, put on your clothes, eat your rice, pass the time doing nothing."[15] This type of religion and ethics is paradoxical or *negative* religion and ethics. It is not geared toward lofty ideas and ideals, to elevated states of mind, but to a reduction of mental and social aspirations that create artificial stress, delusions, and tensions. It tries to establish a state that is not so different from what Aristotle called calmness. And one of the main obstacles to being in this state is the ethical mindset, the emotionally charged morality of anger. Such anger makes it difficult to simply pass the time doing nothing, to say nothing of trying to sleep. A morality of anger, along with other emotional and social excitements, does not reduce suffering. It is, on the contrary, among the greatest impediments to what the Zen Buddhist conceived of as (paradoxical) enlightenment.

It is important to reiterate that the Zen Buddhists, unlike the Christians, do not advocate replacing the hatred of evil with unconditional love. In fact, the preoccupation with love is as much a part of what Huihai called wrong thinking as hate. One does not naturally love everything and everyone, and particularly not those who, for instance, commit crimes. To replace a morality of anger with a morality of love does not reduce one's level of emotional delusion and excitement. It does not contribute to bringing about calmness.

I think the Zen Buddhists were right in assuming that unconditional love is not the solution to hate and anger, and that to think in terms of good is not the solution to thinking in terms of bad and evil. I do not know if a completely calm state of mind, such as Zen Buddhist enlightenment, is achievable or even desirable, but I certainly think that their vision implies a valid criticism of the morality of anger. The morality of anger functions like a perpetual love-hate game, a good vs. evil dialectics that leads to an emotional and social chain reaction. Once one begins to think, feel, and act in moral terms it is hard to stop. Once you start conceiving of someone else as evil it is difficult to change your mind. It is a simple truism that all kinds of ethnic, political, and other social conflicts are hard to resolve because the parties involved have been accustomed to this morality of anger. A Christian might argue that the conflicting parties should be admonished to love each other, but the empirical results of such an approach are not very encouraging. I think that a negative ethics that simply aims at letting go of a morality of anger without attempting to substitute it with its opposite is probably more practical.

Walter Berns' celebration of moral anger is, in my view, a good example of the problem of morality. It nurtures the love-hate game and easily gives rise to a vendetta-like mental disposition and social climate. The particular American moral heroism advocated by him might be attractive to moviegoers and may be effective as a rhetorical social weapon to persuade people to think and act aggressively—as outlined by Aristotle. I strongly doubt, however, that it is more useful than disengaged means, such as, for instance, legal ones, to deal with conflict. Berns' morality of anger perpetuates the emotions of love and hate so well described by the Aristotelian dialectic of emotional pain and pleasure. It aims at revenge and retribution.

The model of negative ethics has an entirely different conception of mental and social relief and tries to break altogether with such a dialectics. In Berns' model, the function of the law is to restore the mental well-being of the victim by punishing the offender. Contrarily, from the perspective of negative ethics, the benefit of the law is that the legal system, an impersonal institution, takes charge of the case and thus relieves the victim of a crime from the need to seek for revenge.

In most cases where one starts thinking in terms of a morality of anger, there is no legal solution to the issue. Still, it is doubtful that being righteously angry with your obnoxious colleague or family member is more beneficial than avoiding such a mindset. It is certainly sometimes hard to avoid but is still much easier to realize than the Christian model of unconditional love. Generally speaking, it is less demanding, and, I believe, mentally and socially healthier, to be a Zen Buddhist antihero than a Bernsian hero of anger or a Christian hero of love.

5 | ETHICS AND AESTHETICS

THE DEFENDANTS OF a morality of anger praise ethics for con-
tributing to personal and social health. The Zen Buddhists dispute
such a view and so do the Daoists. While the Zen Buddhists focus
their criticism on the obstacles for attaining enlightenment that are
created by a moral mindset, the Daoists tend to highlight other
problems. One of the criticisms of ethics brought forward by the
Daoists can, from a contemporary perspective, be called an aesthetic
objection. In the *Zhuangzi* a legendary sage named Xu You appears
as a Daoist spokesman. When Xu You is approached by a man who
has just visited the sage ruler Yao, that is, the Confucian model of
morality, the following dialogue occurs:

Xu You [the Daoist master] said [to Yi Erzi, the man approaching
him]: "What kind of assistance has Yao [the Confucian sage and
model of morality] been giving you?"

Yi Erzi said: "Yao told me: 'You must learn to practice benevolence and righteousness and to speak clearly about right and wrong.'"

"Then why come to see *me*?" said Xu You. "Yao has already tat-
tooed you with benevolence and righteousness and cut off your
nose with right and wrong. Now how do you expect to go wandering in any far-away, carefree, and as-you-like-it paths?"

"That may be," said Yi Erzi. "But I would like, if I may, to wander
in a little corner of them."

"Impossible!" said Xu You. "Eyes that are blind have no way to tell the loveliness of faces and features, eyes with no pupils have no way to tell the beauty of colored and embroidered silks."[1]

The Daoist master clearly regards instructing someone who has been "infected" with Confucian morality as hopeless. He compares this exposure to morality with the bodily mutilation inflicted by ancient Chinese legal punishment: tattooing the skin and cutting off the nose. From a Daoist point of view, such a mutilation prevents people from taking the course of the Daoist way, the so-called wandering in any far-away, carefree, and as-you-like-it paths. Distinguishing between right and wrong is compared to being blind or having eyes without pupils and therefore being unable "to tell the loveliness of faces and features" and "the beauty of colored and embroidered silks." Once harmed by a moral outlook, one has become truly—in the literal sense of the word—*in-sane*.

The moral distinction—the ability "to speak clearly of right and wrong"—is conceived of as a distinction superimposed on more basic features such as certain natural or aesthetic qualities that enable us to recognize things like lovely faces and beautiful materials. It is portrayed as an unnecessary and secondary distinction that blurs our perception of the world and irritates our behavior. One who thinks and acts morally is already too spoiled to become a Daoist.

Nature is neither good nor evil. Animals, plants, and stones cannot be measured by these categories. It is not evil or bad for one animal to kill and eat another or for a plant to die. If one attempts to appreciate the way of nature, that is, the Dao, a moralist outlook will be counterproductive. There is no morality involved in the cosmic process of production and reproduction. Moral categories seem to be a peculiar human construct and do not contribute much to a broader and nonanthropocentric awareness of one's environment. The loveliness of the features of nature and the nature of faces cannot be grasped ethically.

The above passage from the *Zhuangzi* extends its criticism of ethics to the realm of aesthetics. The beauty of nature, as well as the beauty of artifacts—such as embroidered silk—is nonethical. The appreciation of aesthetic beauty and the application of moral categories are at odds with one another. There does not appear to be any correlation (either positive or negative) between ethical and aesthetic judgments or perceptions.

The incompatibility of ethical and aesthetical perceptions is rather obvious with respect to artifacts and visual arts or music. A beautiful dress, an interesting sculpture, or a fascinating symphony is normally not evaluated in ethical terms—and if it is, this is often perceived as odd, pathological, or even criminal. One may think of the destruction of evil Buddhist sculptures in Afghanistan or of the proscription of certain improper pieces of classical music under Stalin. These acts were commonly criticized as fanatical vandalism or ideological lunacy. Similarly, the ethical and political embracing of certain aesthetic styles and forms, as, for instance, in Nazi Germany or, again, under Stalin, with respect to architecture, mass celebrations, and sculpture is often seen as suspect—to say the least. It is then seen as some sort of liberation if, for example, paintings in the style of socialist realism can finally be appreciated *without* looking at them as representations of ethically endorsed (or mandated) lifestyles, personalities, and character traits.

Another genre of art, however, is quite commonly analyzed in moral terms. It does not seem odd to apply ethical criteria when evaluating a novel or a movie. Films and books are often said to be morally educating, that is, to have ethical value. A philosophical advocate of an ethical aesthetics, at least with respect to literature, was Richard Rorty.

One of the postmodern aspects of Richard Rorty's philosophy is his embrace of literature and, consequently, his departure from traditional Western conceptions of philosophy as a science. Rorty celebrates the narrative function of both philosophy and literature, and emphasizes, particularly in *Contingency, Irony, and Solidarity*, their crucial importance for realizing personal individuality, social pluralism, and political liberalism. Rorty advocates a "conversational philosophy" that aims at "enlarging our repertoire of individual and cultural self-descriptions" and helping "us grow up—to make us happier, freer, and more flexible."[2] For him, both literature and philosophy are creative projects of authorship that describe the world anew, tell a new narrative, and invite people to converse about it so that they and their culture can undergo further transformation. Seen in this way, it is obvious that, for Rorty, philosophy cannot be essentially distinguished from literature. Both disciplines produce texts and tell stories. Literature and philosophy may differ in style, but their purpose within a broader literary culture is similar. They both fulfill social and educational functions that tie them to Rorty's ethical-pragmatist project. If philosophy is not so much an objective science that increases knowledge, but a discourse among people, then its effects are consequently not so much scientific as ethical.

Authors of philosophy and literature can either represent the struggle for private and idiosyncratic self-perfection—Rorty names Plato, Heidegger, Proust, Nabokov, and others as examples—or they can further the perfection of society—here he names writers such as Dickens, Mill, Dewey, Orwell, Habermas, and Rawls.[3] Thus, literature and philosophy are either means of gaining personal autonomy or tools for bringing about social cohesion, freedom, and the absence of violence.[4] For Rorty they function aesthetically and ethically at the same time. From his perspective, art and morality are perfectly matched, at least when it comes to literature. They contribute equally to the pragmatist project of morally improving society.

Literary texts (in the broadest sense that includes all sorts of narrative genres) can be simultaneously perceived aesthetically and ethically. Many people believe that literature morally educates and that it is an excellent means for conveying cultural values. It is pointless to deny this and to state that aesthetics and ethics have nothing to do with one another. Thus, the Daoist view taken on by Xu You in the passage quoted above seems to be too radical—or at least untenable in our society where narratives play such an important role in the mass media and thus contribute significantly to the dissemination of moral norms among the population. At least with respect to novels and movies, there seems to be a tight connection between ethics and aesthetics.

I look somewhat closer at the relation between narrative and morality—and thus between ethics and aesthetics—in this chapter. I criticize, at least implicitly, Rorty's view on the educational and pragmatic role of literature in creating a better society and try to suggest a less idealistic, or optimistic, and a more dialectical evaluation of the function of morality in literature and its social effects. First, I discuss literary works that are, in my view, *not* ethical at all, or at least not primarily ethical. Second, I discuss literary works that clearly have an ethical dimension and deal with ethical issues, but I argue that what makes them aesthetically interesting is not their morality. Third, I look at ethical narratives that present a noncomplex or *simplistic* morality. And, finally, I look at narratives that present *complex* ethical problems. I rely mainly on examples from literature but, sharing Rorty's broad understanding of literature, also talk about other media.

Many literary works, regardless of whether they are great books, have no particular ethical relevance. Or, to say the least, they do not *need* to be understood in an ethical way. The novels of Proust and Kafka, for instance, do not (in most cases) present moral questions to their readers. This does not preclude the possibility for professional analysts and professors of literature to come up with an ethical reading of these texts—obviously, an interpretation can, legitimately, do anything with a given text—but I would still claim that a story like Kafka's *Metamorphosis* can be read without identifying any moral meaning. Modern literature, with Kafka as a prime example (and Thomas Pynchon a more contemporary, but equally eminent one), experiments with all kinds of intricate psychological states and complex narrative structures that cannot be readily reduced to a specific ethical message. While there are perhaps some evil or dark figures in Kafka, they can hardly be understood as characters in the traditional sense. They are not realistic enough (or are too surreal) to be seen as an artistic illustration of a specific moral problem. To think of these figures in ethical terms is as problematic as thinking of animals in ethical terms. The context in which they act is too far removed from the social contexts in which we normally apply ethical and moral judgments. Kafka's novels do not correspond in any obvious way to the social scenarios that make moral categories relevant.

One does not have to restrict this nonethical reading to modern literature. Classical novels by writers such as Miguel de Cervantes or Laurence Sterne also clearly transcend moral issues. Again, this does not preclude finding an ethical dimension in these writings, but they have no outright focus on moral issues. Tristram Shandy and

Don Quixote are not obviously good or bad, and they do not ponder moral problems most of the time—and, when they do, they don't do so seriously. Some novels deal primarily with love and passion, and some don't. Similarly, some novels deal primarily with morality and some don't. If literature is seen as ethically educational, as Rorty proposes, one must nonetheless admit that not all literature is (primarily) ethical, and that the ethical value of a work is not immediately correlated to its aesthetic appeal. While there is moral literature, there is also a good deal of amoral literature, and I do not think that the former is necessarily better—ethically, educationally, or pragmatically—than the latter. The moral focus of a novel is, in my mind, not a significant criterion for its aesthetic, social, or cultural evaluation.

I readily admit that some literary works *are* focused on moral issues. A prime example—which Rorty often refers to—is Charles Dickens. Dickens' novels typically revolve around moral issues, and one cannot but divide their characters into goodies and baddies. (But one can also reverse the point made in the preceding paragraphs: The moral surface of Dickens by no means precludes interpretations that do not deal with ethics. Literature that is amoral on the surface can be read morally, and literature that is moral on the surface can be read amorally.) His novels generate moral sympathies and antipathies toward his protagonists. One likes the (often poor and mistreated) young heroes and dislikes the hypocrites and greedy schemers. The tension that evolves within Dickens' stories is typically a moral tension, and the conflicts he portrays are more often than not moral conflicts. His novels manage to fascinate their readers—at least in part—due to the moral passions they generate.

The fact that Dickens' work is typically highly moral is not its sole attraction. There is much literature that is equally ethical but does not garner the same enthusiasm and praise from readers and critics. The sheer morality of the stories is not sufficient or necessary to make them aesthetically interesting. A nineteenth-century treatise on female chastity or against the consumption of alcohol may be as highly moral as *Oliver Twist* but it is unlikely to find many enthusiastic modern readers. It cannot then be the moral views presented by Dickens that contribute primarily to the *aesthetic* appreciation of his work. I would go so far to say that the concrete content of Dickens' nineteenth-century western European ethics is largely *irrelevant* for the ability of his novels to attract readers from all over the world at the beginning of the twenty-first century. Our ethical convictions do not have to overlap with Dickens' in order for us to find his books aesthetically valuable. It certainly does not hurt if we share many of his moral sentiments, but this simple agreement is not sufficient to make us read and reread a book several hundred pages in length.

Many factors contribute to the aesthetic appreciation of a novel by Dickens and I doubt that ethical values rank high among them. I like reading his novels because the plot is always interesting. I want to know what happens next. For me, Dickens' books are page-turners, but this is not because I have a particular interest in his moral views. I also like Dickens' works because of its historical character. Of course, they are not in any way scientific studies of nineteenth-century England (and the United States), but they still bring, however artificially, another time to life. It is fascinating to be drawn into this world that one has no way of experiencing firsthand. Reading a novel by Dickens can be as interesting as traveling to a foreign country. One enjoys a different world. These aspects—and many others—are more important for my aesthetic admiration of Dickens than his morals.

Still, I have not yet addressed the main problem that I have with an ethical reading of moral literature. While I agree that some fascinating novels—such as those by Dickens—are indeed moralist, I do not believe that they necessarily educate their readers morally. I know of no empirical study that has investigated this, but I doubt that readers of Dickens (and this includes me) are morally superior to those who haven't read him (or other moralist writers). I also doubt that the world became a better place after Dickens or that it would be ethically poorer if we didn't have his work. Dickens' main literary thrust is morality, but, as a great writer, he *plays* with his material. It is not the material as such that counts, but what he does with it. Dickens is a very humorous author and he presents morality in a funny and ironic way. This is what makes his presentation of moral issues aesthetically interesting. I like his books not because they are moral but because of their irony, because they deal playfully with morality. In fact, I enjoy reading about every character while, in reality, I am happy for every minute that I am not exposed to a Mr. Pecksniff.

I would argue that Dickens' novels have such a great appeal because they make morality so much more bearable. They give us a break from its heavy burden and have, I suggest, a cathartic effect. Instead of fretting about all the real Mr. Pecksniffs, we take a holiday from our moral sentiments while we read about him. Dickens' novels attract people not because they are highly moral but because they provide a paradoxical and ironic relief from our moral thinking. In fact, I think that while his novels are moralist on the surface, they function aesthetically in an amoral way. While they deal mainly with ethical issues, they do so in an ironical way so that they become ultimately amoral (but not immoral).

While I think that some great literary works (like Dickens') deal with morality, but are, paradoxically, aesthetically amoral, there are clearly also works that have little to offer beyond their morals. Many novels and films are reduced to the conflict between the good guys and the bad guys and there is simply not much more to their narrative than this conflict and its resolution. After all kinds of adventures the hero finally overcomes the villain and that's all. I think that a good recent example of this type of narrative is found outside of what was traditionally considered as literature, but what may be seen as something like applied literature: video games. They have become increasingly popular, and new releases generate higher sales figures than many blockbuster movies. There are many crossovers between games and movies (e.g., *Tomb Raider* and *Star Wars*) and this alone justifies an understanding of these games as texts or narratives. One may call them a kind of interactive literature.

Many video games are based on the conflict between goodies and baddies, and the players have to identify themselves with the goodies—or, carnivalistically, with the good baddies (this seems to be increasingly the case, one example being *Grand Theft Auto*).[5] This identification, however, goes much further than in traditional literary genres. In the game, one becomes the protagonist and takes on the responsibility for the defeat of the opposition. Video games are thus, in my mind, the most drastic example of ethical literature. They are based on a highly simplistic moral conflict, and they call for a mental and physical participation in the artificial contest between good and evil. In a sense, video games are the successors of religious and moral propaganda texts. Of course, and unlike those other texts, they are meant to be entertaining rather than educational. It came as no surprise to me that there is a popular video game on the market in the United States (*Left Behind: Eternal Forces*) in which one has to either convert or kill anti-Christian people. Such video games and similar films, books, comics, and so on, are, I think, the most influential, the most widespread, and the most simplified forms of moral literature in contemporary society. They are the materials that Rorty should look to when he talks about the educational effects of moral literature—and not Dickens. While Dickens is still read by many, there are certainly many more people who derive their literary education in ethics from very different sources.

It is not at all my intention to demonize video games or pulp fiction (which includes books and films). I am only pointing out that these are, as any look at the world shows, the dominant forms of contemporary moral literature. I do not know if they have a good or bad educational effect—or if they have an effect at all. They typically operate with extremely simplified moral distinctions and are often—at least to me—aesthetically uninteresting. I therefore do not believe that this kind of literature (as Rorty implies) contributes pragmatically to making our society more moral. (But I am not claiming the opposite effect either.) And I also do not think that there is a correlation (positive or negative) between their moral focus and their aesthetic quality.

The final type of moral literature that I discuss concerns narratives that are ethical in nature, but ethical not only on the surface (such as Dickens) or simplistically (such as video games) but also in a complex manner. The examples I have in mind are Dostoevsky's novels. These can indeed be said to focus on moral issues, and certainly not just ironically. (Nonetheless, Dostoevsky is a great master of ironical or carnivalistic prose.) His protagonists are often involved in deeply complex ethical conflicts. The most famous case is probably Rodion Raskolnikov, the antihero of *Crime and Punishment*. This young man commits a murder in cold blood and without the slightest feeling of moral guilt. The novel then describes his increasing moral quarrels with himself and the development of a torn conscience. Clearly, moral issues are not only the stuff that the novel plays with, but also the philosophical (and religious) heart of the story. Books like *Crime and Punishment* are intricate ethical dramas and their aesthetic appeal is tightly interwoven with their subtle illustration of ethical dilemmas.

The important difference between Dostoevsky's narratives and the simplistic moral narratives of many movies and games is that he does not present a clear-cut distinction between the good and the bad. There are moral conflicts, but they tend *not* to take on the shape of a clear black-and-white opposition. His most interesting characters are not simply good or evil, and the reader cannot easily discern what is right and what is wrong. In fact, most of Dostoevsky's great novels do not end with a solution to the ethical conflicts. In the simplistic works of moral pulp fiction, the heroes will win and the villains will lose, so that, in the end, the ethical equilibrium is reestablished. The good and the bad have been firmly distinguished and receive the appropriate reward or retribution. Dostoevsky's novels typically do not have such endings; in fact, they often seem to me to have no conventional ending at all. At a certain point the story breaks off, and Dostoevsky adds a final chapter that briefly wraps up the plot and relates what happens during the rest of the characters' lives. These pseudoendings indicate, in my view, Dostoevsky's reluctance to decide the ethical dilemmas he has presented. The very complexity of Dostoevsky's moral cases precludes a simple decision. At the end, the reader does not know what exactly is good or bad. Dostoevsky does not educate his readers by pointing out what kind of behavior is ultimately right and what, ultimately wrong. There is no simple moral in his novels. They do not provide concrete ethical guidelines or answers questions about how to live. They only present, in an extremely refined aesthetical form, the problems of morality.

While novels such as Dostoevsky's are clearly ethical, and in my view, their aesthetic appeal has much to do with their ethical substance, I would still argue that they cannot be reduced to an ethical message. In this sense, they are not morally educating. If they were, like many simplistic texts of moral fiction, they would lose their aesthetic attraction. One does not—or at least I do not—enjoy reading *Crime and Punishment* because Raskolnikov is finally "brought to justice." This novel is not a moral treatise but a meditation on the complex ambivalence of crime and punishment and of ethical and religious issues.

I dare to contradict Richard Rorty's claim that literature (as well as philosophy) is, or should or could be, ethically educational and thus contribute pragmatically to promoting morality within a society. I think that aesthetics and ethics are, in most cases, quite distinct from one another. One normally does not take delight in nature for ethical reasons. Similarly, one often enjoys works of art regardless of their ethical merits. With respect to literature, the case is more complicated. There are various ways in which ethical issues play a role in literature, and I attempt to outline some of these in this chapter. In the end, my point is that literature does *not* ethically educate in Rorty's sense. There are some literary works such as Dostoevsky's novels that may be ethically rewarding, but they do not promote moral behavior in a pragmatic sense. I do not think that reading Dostoevsky (or Dickens) contributes significantly to one's moral goodness. It certainly contributes to one's ability to reflect on ethical problems and to gain a better understanding of the subtleties of moral dilemmas and conflicts, but there is a great difference between the ability to see deeper into moral issues and being a good person. Rorty ascribes to literature the nearly magical function of being able to create better people. I am not so sure that it does.

If literature functions ethically in society—even through video games and Hollywood movies—I am not sure that this should be called educational (in Rorty's sense). The simplistic distinctions taught by popular narratives are, I think, much more indicative of the pathologies of ethics than a pragmatic contribution to a better society. They certainly teach people how to make rigid distinctions between good and evil, and one of the main effects of the mass media is, I believe, the continuous impregnation of society with morality. However, I do not see at all why this is necessarily a good thing. The present book is concerned with questioning the goodness of moral distinctions and moral language. In part, this questioning relates to works of art and literature. I do not see how any work of art or narrative would gain aesthetically by introducing moral distinctions. And I also do not see how society would necessarily benefit from such a moral aesthetics.

In the end, I hope I have defended the old Daoist master Xu You. I agree with his amoral aesthetics. For the most part, moral categories are not helpful when it comes to aesthetics. An ethical outlook does not make it easier, but rather much harder, to appreciate nature and art. One is better off, I believe, to leave ethical considerations behind when enjoying art or scenery. While some works of art, and especially narratives, involve moral issues, it is still possible, and I contend more appropriate, to view these amorally instead of on the basis of ethical convictions.

6 | THE PRESUMPTIONS
OF PHILOSOPHICAL ETHICS

THERE IS CURRENTLY a boom in an interest in ethics, and my professional field—academic philosophy—is by no means an exception. Ethics is probably the most popular area in philosophy, certainly among those that offer the best chance of employment. This is, of course, nothing new. Ethics has always been one of the main strands of Western philosophy ever since its beginnings in ancient Greece. Still, I would argue, there is a specific reason why philosophical ethics is nowadays so in vogue. Traditionally, Western philosophy was generally conceived of, and conceived of itself, as the most fundamental academic discipline, as the source of all valuable knowledge about humans and the world. The natural sciences as well as many social sciences, and, of course, fields in the humanities, had their place in philosophy and were seen as an integral part of it. This is no longer the case. Today no one considers it necessary to study Plato or Aristotle in order to become a physicist, biologist, or even psychologist. When all these disciplines gained practical applicability, academic independency, and public prestige through their separation from philosophy, the prestige of philosophy shrank. Many people in contemporary North American society have no idea whatsoever what philosophy is about—nor what it is "good for." While most people also have no clue about what exactly academic physicists or psychologists do, they normally assume that they are doing something useful and practical. Accordingly, these fields are able not only to sustain their social esteem but also their public and private funding. This is not the case when it comes to the humanities, and particularly when it comes to philosophy. Ethics seems to be if not the only, then, at least, the most promising, field within philosophy that can pretend to be useful and thus gain recognition and public funds. Few people know or understand what analytic philosophers of language and experts on the history of Continental philosophy actually do and would probably not be particularly enthusiastic about funding them with their tax dollars if they did know. The situation is different with regard to ethics, and this is why it is so important—at least for the survival of academic philosophy.

Ethics is the most applicable field in philosophy. Look at any course calendar to see a list of its multiplying branches: bioethics, environmental ethics, business ethics, and so on. All these areas can be sold to financing agencies, the administration, the media, and students. They give the impression that they actually contribute to social progress, to a better world, to the public good. All professional philosophers should be grateful to ethics. It allows them to do whatever they do as long as the ethicists shield them from the public eye. Without ethics, the phenomenologists and the experts on Frege would likely be in trouble. Thus both the public and the philosophical profession profit from ethics. The public can happily assume that there are experts who research what is good—and who would not want to know this or at least make some scientific progress toward it? We can be assured that there are people who take care of discovering, protecting, and distributing values in society. The philosophers, on the other hand, can claim that they are in fact useful and therefore need to be given good salaries and plenty of time to read and write books—or do whatever else they do. Being a professional philosopher myself, I often feel that my social status is somewhat similar to that of the cleric in medieval times. No one is really sure what exactly my services consist of, but there is a consensus that it must be something valuable and important, that I deserve to be well paid to teach the young, and that I should be allowed to spend most of my time not producing anything tangible.

There are at present an abundance of philosophical ethics and it would be tiring and confusing to even attempt a list here. Instead, I focus on two moral philosophers who are, in my view, indicative of what ethicists do and attempt to achieve. They are two founding fathers of modern moral philosophy and among the most influential figures in contemporary Western ethics. There are, of course, many others of considerable importance, but I believe that these two deserve special consideration. I think their approach to moral philosophy is quite symptomatic of what has become of Western ethics and what it presumes to be able to achieve. The two philosophers are Jeremy Bentham and Immanuel Kant. Having these two in mind, Niklas Luhmann stated: "The ethics of utilitarianism and of transcendental theory both aimed at a rational or (in the exceptional German case) a reasonable justification of moral judgments."[1] Modern Western ethics set out to rationally determine what is good or the conditions for what is to be considered good. Many different answers have been given. Still, I think that one does not need to look far to see that the project has been a grotesque disappointment. The epistemological optimism regarding the possibility of constructing a universally valid ethics proved to be unwarranted. Empirically speaking, Luhmann says, academic ethics have failed.[2] I agree.

The basic problem with academic ethics—and, in particular, with their modern founding fathers—is that it pretends to be a *scientific* endeavor. It pretends to be able to do actual research on values and norms of behavior and to come up with concrete suggestions of what to do. "What should we do?" is, according to Kant, one of the basic questions of philosophy, and many philosophers have thought and still think that they can come up with definite answers to that question. Ethicists thus typically conceive of themselves not so differently as, let's say, researchers on traffic who find out how to create a safe and speedy transportation infrastructure. Traffic researchers' efforts have led to some quite impressive results. Transit in developed Western countries usually functions surprisingly well (see the introduction for more about this). People by and large obey the same rules and follow the same instructions—and everybody is more or less happy with the results. The same thing cannot be said about academic ethics. The scientific truths established by Kant, Bentham, and others are not actually practiced systematically in society. Here and there people follow some rules (often not even knowing that such rules exist); some people even turn to academic ethicists to justify what they do; but no specific set of ethics actually test for the categorical imperative is, according to Kant, a purely rational test of the "universalizability" of any given practical "maxim." If it is universalizable, it is morally sanctioned, if not, then not. The test seems to be free of any empirical conditions and proves the rightness or wrongness of a maxim once and for all.

Hegel was, in his *Phenomenology of Spirit*, among the first to come up with a thorough criticism of the categorical imperative. In the section "Reason as Testing Laws" he discusses the issue of private property. Is it OK to steal? Well, if one assumes that private property is a good thing, then obviously not. I cannot say "it is good for me to steal" because this would be self-contradictory. I would, on the one hand, claim the right to private property for myself and deny it to others. But why is private property a good thing in the first place? This is a specific cultural and historical assumption. In a society that does not acknowledge private property, there is nothing wrong with using objects that do not belong to me. One focus of Hegel's critique is that the supposedly categorical character of Kant's moral imperative makes it empty and inapplicable. It is supposed to be totally pure of empirical conditions but there are no ethics outside of empirical conditions. Once there is a moral question, it is always within an empirical context. And if one abstracts from all empirical conditions (such as the existence or nonexistence of private property in a society) then one cannot perform Kant's test at all. In order to perform the supposedly pure test, we always have to adduce some sort of empirical context. Hegel concludes: "It is not, therefore, because I find something is not self-contradictory that it is right; on the contrary it is right because it is what is right."[7] Kant's German purity law of ethics itself seems to be quite contradictory. It pretends not to be historically and culturally contingent, whereas, in fact, it *has* to be.

My main concern with Kant's puritan ethics, however, is not that it is philosophically unsound. I am more worried by the actual ethical prescriptions that Kant arrived at on the basis of the categorical imperative. It is most troublesome to see, on the one hand, Kant's insistence on the purity and scientific necessity of his ethics and, on the other hand, the actual ethical guidelines he comes up with. What is most bizarre and grotesque about Kant's ethical system is

guides our behavior in the way that traffic rules and regulations guide how most people in North America and Europe drive. There is a huge gap between the normative claims of ethicists and the actual application of these claims in society. While many branches of ethics call themselves applied and while there are certainly quite a few people who take the findings of these academic efforts seriously, it cannot be said that we have an overarching, generally accepted and practiced set of scientifically established and proven ethics that the population follows on the whole. People certainly consider themselves to behave ethically—and criticize others for not doing so—but there are no identifiable ethical policies or principles established by a specific school of ethics that are generally acknowledged to be the right ones. Neither the Kantian transcendental theory nor Bentham's utilitarianism is actually the foundation for how most people in our society act or for what they believe is good. The average person does not follow a specific system of ethical rules. Unlike traffic scientists, applied ethicists have failed to successfully apply their rules and norms. Certainly, all kinds of professional ethical codes today are influenced by various ethical philosophies, but there is no one scientific moral system (like Kant's or Bentham's) that is generally practiced. Philosophers like Kant and Bentham stated that they had identified *the* basic principles for good behavior that, if applied, would bring about a scientifically founded good society. Their assertions, however, turned out to be overly optimistic. Some of their rules and norms are followed (and were probably followed long before they were formulated), but their respective claims to have scientifically identified *the* definite principles of how to act seem rather presumptuous.

Kant titled the concise summary of his transcendental philosophy the *Prolegomena to Any Future Metaphysics That Will Be Able to Present Itself as Science*. He believed—like many other philosophers have—that he had finally managed to turn philosophy into a real science. The principles and axioms he had found were not some idiosyncratic inventions and constructions, but actual scientific truths—not so different, for instance, from the truths discovered by physicists, only *more* fundamental and reasonable. He also clearly believed that after him, any philosophy (that could justifiably claim to be scientific) would have to be based on his own as *the* scientific paradigm. This turned out be quite a presumptuous prediction. Kant's scientific metaphysics includes not only the analysis of pure reason but also the analysis of practical reason. Besides the *Critique of Practical Reason*, he published *Grounding for the Metaphysics of Morals* and *The Metaphysics of Morals*, which outline his moral science.

Kant explicitly states in the first paragraphs of the preface to *Grounding for the Metaphysics of Morals* that he considers his moral philosophy to be *scientific*. According to him, ethics is the science of the laws of freedom.[3] It is the science of how to make correct use of our own free will to establish a society based on reason. There is only one reason, and, accordingly, only one reasonable set of ethical rules. Reason is not historical or culturally relative. Strictly speaking, reason has no history and knows no cultural difference. Reason is universal, and if we are able to scientifically understand reason, we will be able to come up with definite guidelines for living reasonably. Kant believed that he had discovered the fundamental principles of reason and reasonable behavior and was thus showing to the world, for once and for all, what can truly be called good and evil. He believed he had found the scientific answer to the perennial question: "What are we to do?"

Kant distinguishes clearly between empirical philosophy and science, which deals with actual experience, and what he calls *pure* philosophy, which deals not with actual experience but (if it is not merely formal) with reason and understanding alone. Pure reason is transcendental reason, reason that precedes experience. It is reason that is not yet, so to speak, soiled by experience. It is the basic structure of reason that enables us to have experience in the first place. Kant's aim in his moral philosophy is to come up with a moral metaphysics that "must be carefully purified of everything empirical . . . a pure moral philosophy that is wholly cleared of everything which can only be empirical and can only belong to anthropology."[4] This means that the principles of morality have nothing to do with empirical conditions, such as cultural or historical conditions (the science of anthropology would have to take care of these), but are principles that precede any concrete empirical situation. These principles are purely reasonable. They follow unambiguously and necessarily from an analysis of reason alone. Once we understand how reason works— independently and prior to its application in life—we will be able to

determine how to use it to guide our behavior. A scientific ethics is concerned with identifying how reason works and what is reasonable *independent* of any concrete situation. By doing so it will be able to define the only reasonable way of acting in the world. Kant is, as usual, very apodictic about this: "All moral philosophy rests entirely on its pure part."[5] Everything that we can scientifically establish about how to act in a truly good way must be based *exclusively* on the scientific analysis and understanding of reason, a reason untouched by anything empirical.

Kant was obsessed with purity. To me, he is the philosophical equivalent of those who suffer from an obsessive compulsion to clean their hands continuously and are afraid to touch anything that has not been disinfected. He believed in the absolute cleansing of ethics—and I am quite alarmed when it comes to such visions. The homeland I share with Kant has a quite problematic historical record with respect to applied cleansings.

Kant not only believed in the complete purity of his ethics, but also in its scientific nature. Being scientific it was the only feasible ethics and hence, the only possible and absolutely necessary foundation for a good society. This is the reason why he says: "A metaphysics of morals is thus indispensably necessary."[6] Kant had discovered the true structure of reason, and any account that substantially differed from his own had to be wrong. He believed his ethical findings to be as solid as the law of gravity.

The basic ethical principle identified and "discovered" by Kant is, of course, the categorical imperative. The better known of its two famous formulations is found in section 7 of the *Critique of Practical Reason*. It is, in Kant's words, the "foundational law of pure practical reason," and it states that one should act in such a way that the maxim of one's will can always be held as a principle of common law. The categorical imperative basically says that the maxim of one's action should not be self-contradictory. I cannot reasonably say it is good for me to lie, for instance, because I would then also implicitly state that it is good for everybody to lie. This would cause the very concept of lying to become meaningless because the distinction between truthfulness and nontruthfulness would have been undermined. The maxim "it is OK to lie" is therefore self-refuting and has, for purely rational reasons, to be classified as immoral. The

the obvious gap between its scientific and universalist attitude and the actual moral teachings he bequeathed us.

I discuss four concrete examples from *The Metaphysics of Morals*: his views on sex, servants, the death penalty, and the killing of illegitimate children. Before I do this I stress once more that Kant considered the following examples to be absolutely scientific. They are meant to be based solely on rational and reasonable analysis and absolutely pure or devoid of any cultural or historical contingencies. They are meant to be scientifically valid for every rational human being at any time and any place—including the readers of this book.

In a chapter on marriage, Kant points out that "sexual union" consists in "the reciprocal use that one human being makes of the sexual organs and capacities of another." He further notes that this use can either be "natural" or "unnatural," the first meaning heterosexual sex and the latter homosexuality and sex with animals. The latter are "unmentionable vices" for which "there are no limitations or exceptions whatsoever that can save them from being repudiated completely." Homosexuality is, "categorically," the same as having sex with animals—and there is absolutely no way to make it socially or morally acceptable. It must be deemed extremely immoral. Similarly immoral is, as Kant concludes soon after, premarital or extramarital sex. If people want to have sex they "*must* necessarily marry." Premarital or extramarital sex (even if heterosexual) is gravely unethical and a violation of universally and scientifically valid moral principles.[8]

We also learn a little further on that "servants are included in what belongs to the head of a household and, as far as the form (the *way of his being in possession*) is concerned, they are his by a right that is like a right to a thing; for if they run away from him he can bring them back in his control by his unilateral choice."[9] According to Kant, it is scientifically established that, morally, we can own servants as we own objects and that it is perfectly ethical to hunt them down if they flee.

Kant also instructs us about the morality of punishment. Penal law, according to him, is firmly grounded in moral principles. Very much like Walter Berns, Kant argues that killing certain criminals is morally necessary.[10] Kant says that "every murderer—anyone who commits murder, orders it, or is an accomplice in it—must suffer death." The death penalty is, as Kant hastens to add "in accordance with universal laws that are grounded a priori." Obviously, many countries in the world, including Canada and most of Europe, are highly immoral and unreasonable because they have outlawed the death penalty. Even legal practice in the United States is not fully acceptable since, even there, not *every* murderer is condemned to death. Given the relatively small number of death sentences in most countries, the world has been violating on a large scale some of the most basic universal ethical principles—with the noteworthy exception, one might add, of the Taliban, (Perhaps the Taliban had some Kantian ethical advisors for their legal policies.) To stress that the death penalty is universally mandatory Kant gives the following example: "If a people inhabiting an island decided to separate and disperse throughout the world, the last murderer remaining in prison would first have to be executed, so that each has done to him what his deeds deserve." The death penalty is a "metaphysical" duty that cannot be neglected, even if it makes no practical sense. It is a necessary moral cleansing.[11]

Interestingly, Kant mentions a particular exemption, a case where killing does not constitute a murder, and in which, therefore, the death penalty is not called for. This case is a mother's killing of a child born out of wedlock. Kant once more instructs us about the scientific moral evaluation of such a case: "A child that comes into the world apart from marriage is born outside the law (for the law is marriage) and therefore outside the protection of the law. It has, as it were, stolen into the commonwealth (like contraband merchandise), so that the commonwealth can ignore its existence (since it rightly should not have come to exist in this way), and can therefore also ignore its annihilation." "Illegitimate" children, have, according to pure and universal moral principles, the status of "contraband merchandise," and therefore their mothers can "annihilate" them without having to fear they will be accused of murder.[12]

These examples clearly illustrate, in my view, how *grotesque* Kantian moral philosophy is. It pretends to scientifically identify universal moral principles based on pure reason. The outcome of these principles, however, is nothing but a crude affirmation of the dominating morals of Kant's time and culture—phrased in an extremely pompous pseudoscientific and pseudolegal jargon. It is not my intention to discuss the immorality of Kant's views on sex, servants, the death penalty, and the killing of children by single mothers—my point of view is not a moral one. What I intend to show is Kant's incredible philosophical arrogance. Kant's ethical views are obviously not universal nor based only on pure reason. Since this is the case, his whole ethical system is a monstrous failure. And it proves one of the main claims of this book: Ethics are potentially harmful and can easily lead to social conflict and the use of violence. With such a moral philosophy one can scientifically prove that homosexuals and people who have sex outside of marriage have to be morally and legally condemned, that all murderers and their accomplices must be legally killed, and that certain children can be "annihilated." Reading Kant, I cannot but think of the Zen Buddhist Linji and what he said about philosophical moralists: "There's a bunch of fellows who can't tell good from bad but poke around in the scriptural teachings, hazard a guess here and there, and come up with an idea in words, as though they took a lump of shit, mushed it around in their mouth, and then spat it out and passed it on to somebody else."[13]

Jeremy Bentham, one of Kant's contemporaries, developed an ethical system that is quite different in content. What Kant and Bentham have in common is their level of presumption. Both claimed to have identified *scientifically* the principles of good and evil. Like Kant, Bentham thought that his insights were universally valid and rational and that the world had to follow his system if it wanted to be truly moral. Both believed they had done the world an important service with the publication of their treatises.

Bentham's "principle of utility" is quite simple and straightforward. I quote the first two sentences from the first chapter of his *Introduction to the Principles of Morals and Legislation*: "Nature has placed mankind under the governance of two sovereign masters, *pain* and *pleasure*. It is for them alone to point out what we ought to do, as well as to determine what we shall do."[14] In the same apodictic manner as Kant, Bentham claims to have identified *the only* principles of any possible scientific ethics. In his case, all ethics have to be derived from evaluations of pain and pleasure. Everything that brings more pleasure than pain is good; everything that does not is evil. The problem, of course, is how to establish what is pleasurable and what not—and for whom. Bentham, however, is not hesitant about his project. His treatise is mainly concerned with how to determine, or, more precisely, to measure, pain and pleasure. His ethics, in the end, are a mathematical ethics that pretend to be able to scientifically calculate pain and pleasure—both for individuals and for society as a whole—and thus to distinguish good from evil in a purely rational way. Unlike Kant, Bentham did not pretend to avoid empirical considerations, but he did believe that he had established the universal scientific principles of morality.

I do not list here the pedantic and often grotesque details of Bentham's analysis or his "felicific calculus" by which happiness can be precisely measured. Interested readers may want to look into this themselves. I suggest such passages as the note on how the weight that "a man [*sic*]" can lift relates to his sensibility for pain and pleasure.[15] (Weight lifting thus becomes an efficient tool for evaluating the moral quality of certain public policies.) Equally interesting is Bentham's scientific consideration of the effect of gender on ethics (via the sensibility for pain and pleasure): "In point of quantity, the sensibility of the female sex appears in general to be greater than that of the male. The health of the female is more delicate than that of the male: in point of strength and hardiness of body, in point of quantity and quality of knowledge, in point of strength of intellectual powers, and firmness of mind, she is commonly inferior: moral, religious, sympathetic, and antipathetic sensibility are commonly stronger in her than in the male."[16]

Again, I am not interested in judging the immorality of such statements. But, as with Kant, I am flabbergasted by how the pseudoscientific nature of Bentham's claims compares with the banality and obvious cultural limitations of what he actually says. There is here the same level of academic pretension that one finds in Kant and the same stereotypical stupidity of many of his actual moral judgments. It has often been said that Bentham's ethical measurements and ideal of "the greatest happiness of the greatest number" could be used for justifying any social arrangement that serves the pleasure of a powerful group. Slavery, for instance, could be deemed good if it inflicts pain only on a social minority (and, if one considers this scientifically, a minority which can be found to be less sensitive to pain on the basis of its ethnicity) and gives great pleasure to a large, and more sensitive, majority.

Bentham was more interested in and much more active than Kant with respect to applied ethics. He wanted to be given the opportunity to shape legislation and for his free market morals to be practiced throughout the world. He tried to persuade the British government to adopt his invention the Panopticon. This prison, based on Bentham's moral science, would be circular in shape so that all cells could be constantly observed from the center of the building. He also took part in the public debates about how to deal with poverty in Britain and, again on the basis of his moral science, "insisted that those unable or unwilling to work for their own subsistence should not be better off than those who did. In addition, he proposed a system of Industry Houses run by a joint-stock company to house the indigent and make provision for them to labour and through labour acquire the virtues of frugality, sobriety, and industry."[17]

More so than Kant, Bentham actively tried to impose his ethical system on others. He presumed that his ethics would establish a morally correct society and that any society must apply his principles in order to become good. The actual substance of his ethical suggestions about prisons and the poor demonstrates once more the potential social dangers of such a fundamentalist ethics. Kant's and Bentham's ethical presumptions were slightly different in character but, in my mind, equally grotesque—and their ethical systems were both monstrous failures.

Notwithstanding their often bizarre moral prescriptions and their pseudoscientific presumptions, Kant and Bentham are still considered to be among the most important and most influential moral philosophers in the modern West. Moral philosophies based on reason or utilitarian principles still flourish inside and outside of academic ethics. But hardly any neo- or post-Kantian advocates the killing of illegitimate children, and most utilitarians do not operate with the felicific calculus. The proponents of today's philosophical ethics would say that such errors have been corrected and, thus, that ethics have actually progressed. Our current academic ethics, they could say, may be founded on thinkers like Kant and Bentham, but we have gone beyond them. Our present ethics are much better than our historic predecessors. Why then should I throw out the baby with the bathwater and rail against all academic ethics relying only on some of the peculiar absurdities of philosophers who are long dead?

I am not particularly interested in blaming Kant or Bentham for having come up with wrong or even immoral ethical claims. My prime concern is their presumptuousness, their claim to be able to scientifically establish what is good and bad. In this respect, contemporary Kantian ethicists or utilitarians are not so different. Even today, ethicists often argue that their principles are universally valid. And if they are not ethical universalists, they still normally believe that they are able to identify certain principles and guidelines that should be applied in society. They have the habit of prescribing certain ethical codes to society that are presumed to be academically (and thus, scientifically) valid. I believe, with Wittgenstein, that ethics are inexpressible. And by this I mean that there is no such thing as "moral science." One can, of course, debate what is right and wrong and bring forth good and not so good reasons why this is so. One can have similar arguments with respect to religious or aesthetic values. I do not doubt or deny this. But morality does not seem to be objectively determinable. And if people try to establish scientifically what is good and bad (or, as in the case of Habermas and his followers, the rules for determining rationally what is good and bad), then, it seems to me, this can easily become not only ridiculously grotesque, but also socially dangerous since it easily leads to fundamentalist claims for its application. The same could be said with respect to religious and aesthetic values. Wittgenstein said that if a book were to state conclusively what was right and wrong, all other books would explode.[18] Both Kant and Bentham thought they had written such a book, but so far—in my view, at least—the only books that have exploded are their own.

7 | THE MYTH OF MORAL PROGRESS

IF ONE QUESTIONS the use and goodness of ethics, one is often confronted with objections such as this: Granted, there are problems with a moralistic worldview and there certainly has been some harm done in the name of ethics. Perhaps this harm cannot simply be dismissed as an unfortunate abuse. But has the world not made great or at least significant progress through morality? Haven't we witnessed, in the past few centuries in our part of the world, very important steps forward? Think about the abolition of slavery, for instance, about the more and more encompassing condemnation of religious witch hunts and ethnically motivated genocide. Isn't there much more awareness now in our society about human rights and their inviolability? Obviously, we do not live in a morally perfect world, but we live in a much better one than our grandparents and great-grandparents. Some progress has been made, and this progress is highly important for those who benefit from it (African Americans and women, for example). And more progress is still to come. Rather than denouncing ethics altogether, we should work for more moral progress so that the world will continue to improve.

Such an objection argues historically and assumes an overall ethical development. This position implicitly claims that there is some sort of moral progress; the world seems to morally improve over time—or at least to be capable of such improvement if we only try hard enough. Another version of the hypothesis of ethical development focuses on the individual, not society as a whole. It can be said that human development quite essentially consists in moral development. The older we get, the more moral we become—at least potentially. The more mature we are, the better we are able to think and act ethically. In correspondence with our physical and mental development, we also become more competent ethically. We not only get bigger and smarter, but also better able to make ethical decisions as we age. There seems to be a learning process for morality. Children learn specific moral norms, but, much more importantly, they gradually learn how to conceive of themselves, others, and the world in more refined ethical categories. They become more and more responsible moral agents. This hypothesis therefore claims that individual moral progress is a reality (at least normally). The most famous proponent of this version of moral progress is Lawrence Kohlberg.

I challenge both hypotheses of moral progress in this chapter: first, in a few broad strokes, the general version of historical progress, and then, in a little more detail, the particular version of moral development as presented by Kohlberg.

I have three counterarguments to offer against the hypothesis of historical progress in ethics. The first is logical or rhetorical. It is quite natural but tautological for defenders of any set of ethics to believe that their own system is not only good but also better than all others. If one is convinced of the validity of a certain way of distinguishing between good and evil, then one cannot but affirm that this distinction is the right one. If, therefore, one set of ethics, as, for instance, a set that morally justifies slavery, is replaced by a different set that condemns slavery, then it is self-evident that the second set of ethics will have to claim that it is superior to the previous one. The hypothesis of historical moral progress is then not necessarily self-refuting, but at least self-fulfilling. Any ethical paradigm that is generally accepted in society is accepted simply because it is a generally accepted paradigm. If one believes in the correctness of a generally accepted ethical paradigm, one cannot but believe that it is more advanced than any of the paradigms that have preceded it. Very much in line with Thomas Kuhn's argument on paradigm shifts in the sciences, I would say that there is a history of paradigm shifts in ethics. That a narrative of progress is attached to both histories is rhetorically and logically inevitable, but progress is not an objective fact. Not to believe in the superiority of one's ethical paradigm is impossible. If one did, it would not be one's paradigm. My argument is *not*, to make this as explicit as possible, that condemning slavery is not better than approving of it. In fact, I personally think that it *is* better because I share the antislavery paradigm. But I would say that it is still problematic to infer a theory of moral progress from this. The defenders of slavery were as convinced of the ethical superiority of their position as we are of ours. Our paradigm won, or, to be more precise, we now side with the paradigm that was able to gain general approval. But this has been the case with virtually every paradigm. And it is very problematic, as Kuhn has shown, to conclude that the history of succeeding paradigms is actually a history of progress since there is no neutral vantage point that provides a standard for measuring progress. Our moral values are *our* moral values, and therefore we necessarily believe them to be better than those that are no longer ours.

My second argument against the hypothesis of moral progress in history is discussed in much more detail in chapter 9. I outline it only briefly here. If we look at moral progress from a pragmatic point of view, it seems that the most important progress is made when ethical considerations are transcended—and legal measures take over. What was important for slaves was not that slavery was *morally condemned*, but that it was *legally abolished*. The same is true for all human rights issues. It is debatable how far ethical deliberations are necessary for bringing about legal changes, but, I would argue, the actual *progress* is always more dependent on laws than on ethics. I do not believe in the measurability of ethical or legal values, and thus do not, philosophically, believe in progress in any absolute sense based on any universal or a priori principles. But I would, of course, not deny that I find it better not to be a slave. Such practical change toward the better is, however, effected through laws, not through ethics, and there is no need of transcendent or transcendental ideals for this to occur. Here I agree with Richard Rorty that, from a pragmatic point of view, we do not have to believe in the existence of absolute values and the historical progress toward them in order to be able to distinguish what we like more from what we like less.

Third, I have severe doubts, empirically speaking, that our world has morally improved in the past few centuries—if one applies the ethical criteria of many moralists. For sure, slavery was abolished, human rights were introduced, and so on. This cannot be denied, and, as I have said, from a pragmatic perspective, these changes are good. Still, massive problems have been created along with the supposed moral progress that has been made.[1] Besides the many examples of mass violence, the wars and genocides of the most recent decades, one can think of nonviolent issues, such as, for instance, overpopulation. The world population is growing at such an unprecedented rate that it is not conceivably sustainable. The sheer quantity of growth is so enormous that billions of people can live only under the poorest conditions, and it is likely that this problem will only increase. How moral is it to allow unrestricted growth that leads to great suffering for billions? Perhaps even more ethically problematic is the pollution of the atmosphere that has led to global warming. It seems that the burning of fossil fuels has brought about irreversible climatic changes that may have grave consequences. As it is often said: We may leave a world to our children and grandchildren that is no longer inhabitable—at least not in the way we know. How moral is this? A large portion of the world's natural resources have been exploited in the past two generations. We not only polluted the air by burning oil, we also pretty much used up the oil without any consideration for the needs of future generations. Likewise, we may well have polluted and drained the earth's water resources in such a way that they may no longer be sufficient to supply our drinking water. Even so-called clean energy sources like atomic power are putting a great burden on generations to come who will have to take care of radioactive waste. Let me be clear: I do not propose that these problems should be conceived of as moral problems or should be dealt with morally. What I am saying is that if we look at history in moral terms, it seems difficult to prove that our world is morally better than before.

It is quite problematic to measure our environmental sins against the sins of previous generations (such as slavery), that is, the generations that the proponents of moral progress feel superior to. The argument that our moral sins are much graver than theirs, since we have endangered the very sustainability of human life on the planet, can quite plausibly be made. It could even be argued that we are members of the most immoral society that there has ever been, because this is the first time in history in which human activity can be blamed for substantially damaging the ecosystem of the whole planet. I am, as I said, not making this argument, and I do not have to come up with a standard of ethical measurement since I neither argue for a theory of moral progress nor for one of decline. In fact, I do not think that one can measure and then compare the degrees of the immorality of slavery and pollution. If one argues for moral progress (or decline, for that matter), one would have to come up with such measurements or comparisons. In my view such measurements are absurd.

The core of my argument is that it makes no sense to speak of any general moral progress. We can speak, from a pragmatic perspective, of legal progress (e.g., abolishment of slavery, human rights), but we can certainly also speak, from the same perspective, of environmental decline (e.g., pollution, depletion of resources). If one dares to speak about ethical progress, one would have to take into account all the relevant issues and then try to objectively weigh them. I do not think that this is possible, nor, if it were possible, that it would be very helpful. There is, if my amoral reasoning is correct, no need to look at these problems ethically. As was the case with respect to slavery, what we need is, precisely speaking, not a new environmental ethics, but new environmental laws to deal with the massive problems we face. For this we do not need to know how "evil" CO_2 or the people who are responsible for its emission are, but, for instance, how high these emissions are, what problems they cause, and what restrictions we should impose—and what we should do legally to those who disregard the restrictions. To look at either slavery or the environment in ethical terms may sound nice and give professional ethicists and those who listen to them cozy feelings (and provide for good honorariums), but it is very doubtful that moralizing is of any pragmatic value. It can be argued, again, that ethical considerations necessarily precede legal and other measures, but I doubt that this is so—as I have and will continue to argue. In order to deal with concrete environmental issues we need concrete environmental solutions (new technologies, new regulations, new penalties, new taxes, etc.), not ethical ones. It is unnecessary and unhelpful to look at our environmental problems in terms of good and evil.

I now turn to the idea that moral progress, if not a general historical fact, is at least something that each individual experiences. The psychologist Lawrence Kohlberg outlined a most intricate and detailed model of human moral development. Following the tradition of the developmental psychologist Jean Piaget, Kohlberg investigated empirically the cognitive and behavioral stages that people "normally" go through as they age. Kohlberg and his fellow researchers conducted extensive studies that were aimed at scientifically proving the validity of his basic hypothesis on moral development. This hypothesis concretely consists in a model that distinguishes six stages of moral growth. Starting with a relatively primitive form of moral reasoning, humans gradually establish cognitively more complex types of moral beliefs until they finally reach the highest level of moral capacity—at least potentially. As is not uncommon in empirical psychological research, the studies of Kohlberg and his associates actually did prove the model to be more or less correct. A great number of adjustments were made (such as the introduction of intermediate stages), but they claimed that the hypothesis as such was scientifically sound.

As is also not uncommon in empirical psychological research, not everyone accepted the validity of the hypothesis and other scientists conducted different studies that were meant either to substantially modify Kohlberg's model or to discredit it in part or in whole. I am not a psychologist and not qualified to comment on or evaluate the psychological evidence that was produced to defend or contradict Kohlberg. My intention is to criticize Kohlberg's model from a philosophical point of view. After all, the first volume of his major work, a collection of essays on his theory, is titled *The Philosophy of Moral Development*.[2]

Kohlberg's first stage is called the "stage of punishment and obedience." Morality here consists simply in following blindly, for fear of punishment, the rules imposed on one by an external authority. The second stage is quite utilitarian, or in Kohlberg's terminology, "instrumental" and deems morally right what serves "one's own or others' needs." Stage three is a stage of "conformity" in which one does what one believes is considered "good" by those around one (family, peers, etc.). Stage four includes what Kohlberg calls "conscience maintenance" and differentiates the "societal point of view from interpersonal agreement." It thus considers good what serves the social order in general, not just one's immediate social environment. Stage five is "postconventional" and conceives of moral values a priori. Kohlberg explains that it "takes a prior-to-society perspective" and that individuals here rationally reflect on the validity of moral rights and values. The sixth and final stage is the stage of "universal ethical principles." Here the rational reflection on morality is most encompassing. This "stage assumes guidance by universal ethical principles that all humanity should follow." For people at this stage, the "reason for doing right is that, as a rational person, one has seen the validity of principles and has become committed to them." These people therefore share the perspective "of any rational individual recognizing the nature of morality."[3]

Obviously, these stages are supposed to represent the linear and hierarchical moral improvement that humans can make. Each stage is morally better than the preceding, and one needs to grow older and go through the lower stages in order to get to the higher ones. It is a moral ladder that you climb by aging. The last stage is the ultimate summit of morality. Here one gains insight into the very "nature of morality" and understands the absolute validity of certain principles that any fully rational individual necessarily agrees with. Kohlberg and Mordecai Nisan state: "These features of the development of moral judgment lead to a culturally invariant sequence of stages, or hierarchical organizations, each more differentiated and integrated, and thus more equilibrated, than its predecessor."[4] Clearly, the stages are meant to depict moral progress. They are also believed to be strictly psychological or cognitive and thus culturally invariant. Morality is a cognitive achievement that is independent from culture and culminates in an a priori and universal rationality.

In my view, Kohlberg's model of moral development combines the worst aspects of Kant's and Bentham's ethics. Like Kant's, it claims to have identified an a priori, rational, universal, and culturally invariant morality. And with Bentham, it claims to have identified how to scientifically measure morality. Of course, the actual universal principles that are grasped at Kohlberg's sixth stage are slightly different from Kant's. Kant, living in eighteenth-century Europe, had identified the moral values of his time and place as the universal, rational, and culturally invariant ethical principles (including the moral excuse of killing "illegitimate children"). Kohlberg did most of his work in the 1960s and 1970s and, accordingly, found that the ethics of social justice propagated in the Western world by his generation were rational and culturally invariant. Unlike Bentham, he did not operate with the felicific calculus, but developed a much more contemporary way of quantifying the distinction between good and evil. Because he was a good empirical psychologist, most of his works consist of concrete scientific studies on measures and methods of measuring of morality. Kohlberg's second monumental work is called *The Measurement of Moral Judgment*.[5]

In chapter 6, I argue in detail against the philosophical presumptions of claiming to have identified *the* rational, a priori, universal, and invariant principles of morality and of claiming to be able to scientifically measure these. My arguments are basically identical with respect to psychological theories that presume to make the same claims. I think that Kohlberg's moralist universalism is as misguided as Kant's, and that his measurements are as absurd as Bentham's.

I do not wish to engage here in a polemic against the use of statistics in psychology—or in the social sciences as a whole, for that matter—and I certainly do not accuse Kohlberg of having manipulated his data or misinterpreted the results, or of having used poorly created questionnaires. I do not criticize any of the scientific aspects of his research. Others have done so, but I am not in a position to judge Kohlberg's measurements. I am, however, firmly convinced that Kohlberg did not measure what he thought he was measuring, namely people's moral judgments and, by extension, their moral capacities.

Kohlberg and his associates usually confronted their respondents with a hypothetical ethical dilemma such as: "Your mother is sick, but you can't afford to buy medicine to save her life. Is it OK to steal the medicine?" Then they would ask several questions about what people would do in such a case; if this were to be morally acceptable, how they would justify their actions, and so on. They then compared the answers with the six stages of the model, quantified the results, and made all sorts of evaluations, particularly with respect to age, so that they could measure the moral development of the respondents—or so they assumed. My main objection against this—in my view—pseudomeasurement of morality is that what Kohlberg and his helpers found out was only how certain people replied to certain questions asked by a group of professional psychologists. More specifically, they found out how people responded to hypothetical ethical dilemmas. In other words, what they actually measured was the ability of certain people to communicate on moral issues. No wonder that they found that the answers matched their developmental model. Obviously, adolescents are able to communicate in more complex ways than younger children, and young adults are better able to talk about moral issues than teens. In my view, the results simply show that when faced with a highly hypothetical problem (like that on an English exam at school, for instance), the older you are, the better able you are to express yourself. What they measured was the ability for hypothetical moral communication. They tested how well people had learned to talk morally.

What they did not measure was moral judgment because they would have had to be able to find out how their subjects actually judged real moral issues. Of course, this would have been statistically problematic. It is rather difficult to compare the specific ethical problems people have. How do you measure the moral judgment of someone who cheats on his girlfriend with another who does the

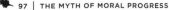

same? The problem is, of course, that they actually do not do the same thing, because each individual case is different and cannot be measured against another. Even if Kohlberg's team had looked at the actual moral judgments of their respondents in real life—how would they pick and choose? Which moral judgment (e.g., cheating on your girlfriend or evading taxes) should be deemed representative? Do we, as individuals, always apply the same principles for judging the moral dilemmas we face? I don't think so. In my experience we judge different cases differently. We normally do not have one set of moral judgments that we consistently apply in every moral dilemma.

Still, if it were possible to somehow measure and identify the moral judgment of a given person at a given age, this still would not measure the moral capacity or the morality of this person. How we *judge* moral issues by no means determines how morally we actually behave. I may well act in a way that most people find quite immoral and nevertheless, if I'm clever enough, come up with very complex moral judgments to justify my behavior. This is done on a continuous basis in politics, before the courts, and also in marriages. The capacity to come up with complex moral judgments is, in my experience, by no means correlated in any significant way with a person's tendency to act in a manner that can be deemed morally good.

Again: What Kohlberg actually measured was how people *in our time* are able to come up with moral communication when they reach a certain age, and not their moral or immoral actions or cognitions. That the results were more or less similar worldwide should not be a surprise in our globalized age. We are all exposed to the global mass media that is the main distributor of moral values (see chapter 11), and we learn how to morally justify our actions through their examples. The act of justifying something morally is an act of communication. Kohlberg ignored the difference between our ability to communicate morally, how we think in ethical categories, and the moral qualities of our actions. The answer to a hypothetical question, in my view, does not say much about how one thinks about moral issues. It is even less indicative of how one would actually behave in a given situation. Therefore, I believe that Kohlberg's scientific measurement of moral judgment is, in the end, not much more useful than Bentham's felicific calculus for measuring morality.

Another major problem I have with Kohlberg's model of moral development is that it pretends, like Kant's categorical imperative, to be a priori and culturally invariant while, at the same time, insisting that it has identified the highest possible form of morality, that is, the most rational and therefore best ethics.[6] Ancient China had a highly developed moral philosophy, namely Confucianism, but Confucian texts hardly look at ethics in terms of universal ethical principles that one follows since "as a rational person, one has seen the[ir] validity."[7] As I see it, for the Confucians, morality had its roots in filial piety (*xiao*), which was based on feeling the appropriate emotions toward one's parents. The whole set of Confucian ethics is based on the emotions one feels toward one's family members. That is to say, it is neither rational nor based on any a priori universal principles. It is, at best, somewhat comparable with Kohlberg's third stage, the so-called stage of mutual interpersonal expectations, relationships, and conformity.

A strict believer in Kohlberg's model is left with two rather problematic options when dealing with non-Western morals such as Confucian ethics. One can first assess Confucianism ethically and rank it at the third stage. But this itself is, in our time, rather unethical. Given the strict hierarchy of Kohlberg's model, this would actually imply that Confucian ethics is underdeveloped and defective. This, in turn, could easily be interpreted as prejudiced, colonialist, and racist. It is not really politically or morally correct to dismiss such an important non-Western moral tradition as ethically immature. In order to save both Kohlberg and Confucianism, only one alternative remains: One has to prove that even Confucianism has an ethics of universal ethical principles. This, however, results in a complete distortion of Confucianism and denies it any ethics other than Kohlberg's.[8] The problem with any ethics that conceives of itself as scientific, universal, and somehow highest is that it has to choose between looking at all other ethics as inferior or denying them any distinct character and substance.

Any ethics that does not correspond with Kohlberg's quite Kantian criteria for the sixth stage necessarily has to be labeled as not as good as an ethics can be. Kohlberg establishes a very strict value difference between the six stages. Little children and infants are thus ethically deficient and underdeveloped. One can only become ethical at a certain age—and, it is implied, will become less so once one's rational capacities begin to decline. Kohlberg's model therefore very much follows the modern Western enlightenment tradition that projects everything that is good on the rationally mature man. Children, women, and the elderly are not fully developed. Though Kohlberg's model does not exclude women from reaching the highest stage, it certainly makes it problematic for children and the elderly to be regarded as highly moral. (This alone makes Confucianism incompatible with Kohlberg, since, for the former, old age deserved the highest respect.) The implication is that humans can only be truly good once they are grown up or fully developed. Everything is measured ethically with respect to its distance from the ideal. One's moral goodness and badness depend on how close one gets to Kohlberg's universal principles.

Kohlberg was quite interested in the social life of the kibbutz and believed that although it was "not an especially warm or emotionally responsive or personal environment," it was quite successful in enhancing the moral development of children.[9] Children mature quite well in the kibbutz, Kohlberg found, and overcome the lower stages of morality relatively quickly. They become morally better at a young age. Kohlberg obviously saw this as an ethical success. The educator A. S. Neill, in the account of his Summerhill school, introduces a different view: "Teachers from Israel have told me of the wonderful community centers there. The school, I'm told, is part of a community whose primary need is hard work. Children of ten, one teacher told me, weep if—as punishment—they are not allowed to dig the garden. If I had a child of ten who wept because he was forbidden to dig potatoes, I should wonder if he were mentally defective. Childhood is playhood; and any community system that ignores that truth is educating in the wrong way. To me the Israeli method is sacrificing young life to economic needs. It may be necessary; but I would not dare to call that system ideal community living."[10]

Although Neill does not talk about moral development in particular, I think his point is a valid criticism of what Kohlberg admires in the kibbutz. Kohlberg's model implies that the sixth stage is better than all preceding stages, and therefore it is good to have one's development geared toward it. All previous stages are deficient. Children are therefore not fully moral and, at age ten, are normally in a stage that is still rather immature. It can thus be seen as good when children, like those in the kibbutz described to Neill, develop moral virtues that are atypical for their age. It is "good" if children want to work for moral reasons because they are obviously morally advanced. From a Kohlbergian standpoint one can praise a system that allows children to get closer to the sixth stage earlier. If one does not share Kohlberg's view, however, and does not believe in the hierarchy of moral stages, then one can find it quite problematic if children are raised "morally" so that they "develop" faster. Neill does not seem to believe in the moral superiority of the rational, grown man who has insight into universal ethical principles. In fact, he seems to imply that children can perhaps profit from an emotionally responsive or personal environment as much as from education in universal morality. And, more importantly, he seems to imply that children do not need to be moral. From Kohlberg's perspective, the younger the child is the worse it is. From Neill's perspective, children are simply amoral and there is no need for them to be otherwise. In fact, it may even be advantageous for children not to be morally spoilt. If this is what Neill had in mind when he wrote that passage, he was quite close to being a Daoist.

A Daoist model for the perfect human being is the infant.[11] One of the qualities, or better, nonqualities, of the infant is that it does not need morality in order to do what is right. The infant is the perfect moral fool. It does what it does naturally and does not look at the world in moral categories. We cannot measure it, and it does not measure us—or anything—in moral terms. It is a fine image of the amoral lifestyle.

I do not discuss the Daoist image of the infant any further here, but I think it is an alternative to Kohlberg's model of moral progress.[12] Not all philosophies look at the rational man who understands universal moral principles as the crown of creation. In fact, some people prefer the company of infants (or even animals) to the company of such men. It is not at all clear to me why the development that Kohlberg delineates should be understood, as he implies, as a development toward something better and better. I do not see why a moral outlook and a moral life is necessarily better and more desirable than an amoral one. Even if people do become more moral as they age—or as I maintain, better qualified to communicate in moral terms—I would still not call this progress. Although I am not advocating a radical Daoist position here and do not suggest that we should all become like infants instead of Kohlberg's moral man, I do hesitate to substantially elevate the latter over the former.

To illustrate my point a bit further I mention the fact that many more acts commonly seen as immoral have been committed by developmentally mature rational people who acted on the basis of supposedly universal principles than by amoral infants. It does not make any sense to claim that the world would actually be better if everyone reached Kohlberg's sixth stage. There is, again, no positive correlation between the ability to justify one's acts morally (which, I agree, an infant is incapable of) and the actual degree of morality in society. It rather seems that the more one is able to justify one's actions morally, the more one is able to justify whatever one does—be it considered moral or immoral. I do not see any empirical evidence for the thesis, implicit in Kohlberg's work, that a world with more people at the sixth stage is preferable to a world with more people at, let's say, the third. It is an empirical fact that teens commit more crimes than children under the age of ten and that people over twenty commit more crimes than teens regardless of their scientifically proven capacity for better moral judgment. If I were sick and had no money, I would be thankful if my son stole the medicine I needed—and I wouldn't care with which of Kohlberg's stages he'd justify what he did. In fact, I'd find it a little more sympathetic if he did it out of love (stage three) than out of a rational understanding of the nature of morality (stage six). But, then again, Kohlberg could rightly object that I haven't reached the sixth stage myself.

Moral progress is a myth, both with respect to history and with respect to individual development. It is somewhat similar to progress in weight loss. We certainly are making a lot of progress in talking rationally about obesity on the basis of universal principles, both as a society and as aging individuals, but we still tend to get fatter and fatter.

31

ETHICS IN CONTEMPORARY SOCIETY

ETHICS IN CONTEMPORARY SOCIETY

8 | FOR THE SEPARATION OF MORALITY AND LAW

IN MY VIEW THERE are two quite effective antidotes for morality, namely, love and law. In chapters 8 through 10, I discuss the latter of these. I argue that laws and the legal system not only have the capacity to function amorally, but that they already do, at least to a certain extent (as has been pointed out by, for instance, William Rasch, Richard Nobles, and David Schiff).[1] And I argue that this is not detrimental, but rather a part of their evolutionary development. That is, the legal system evolved in such a way that it was able to separate itself from morality, and this separation seems to have made it more effective and up to date.

An obvious objection to my defense of the separation of morality and law would follow the line of the argument of the Christian pastor mentioned in the introduction who claimed that a vicious sexual serial killer could only be condemned on the basis of religious (or, more precisely, Christian) values. A secularized version of this argument would be that we do not necessarily need a religious grounding for legal decisions (and prosecutions), but we certainly need an ethical one. We must first come to some sort of agreement on what is "just" in an ethical sense before we can establish a social mechanism that puts justice into practice. Justice seems to be the basic moral value that the legal system subscribes to and uses to justify its existence, powers, and aims. How could one possibly separate the legal system from the moral value of justice? Would this not be entirely paradoxical and against the self-definition of the law?

I see things rather differently. I think that the argument from morality is as misguided—and for basically the same reasons—as the Christian pastor's argument from religion. What they have in common is what could be called a historical fallacy. Both arguments imply that the history of law determines its present state. Both arguments are blind to the evolution of the legal system. While they have some *historical* validity, they both fail to take into account that the times they are a-changin'.

Undeniably, in both Eastern and Western history, law and religion, as well as law and morality, used to be closely interrelated. This is equally true for Confucian China and the civilizations that identified themselves with any of the three Abrahamic religions (Judaism, Christianity, and Islam). All the Abrahamic religions hold a very close relation between the divine and earthly law. Human law tends to be seen either as an immediate divine decree or as an earthly application of divine principles. Most famously, the Ten Commandments represent this kind of inseparability of law and religion. The sharia law that is still practiced today in several countries and communities continues this tradition of identifying sin with crime. It is a crime to kill because killing is against God's will—except in such cases, of course, where killing is declared to be exactly the opposite, namely a religious and, by extension, legal duty that executes the will of God. It should be noted, however, that it is still difficult to say if in such cases religion determines what is law, or if it is perhaps equally possible to see it the other way around. Is the law produced by religious beliefs, or do legal instincts produce certain religious ideas. Instead of hastily attributing a certain status to one or the other, it is perhaps more prudent to simply state that legal and religious beliefs were (and in some cases still are) undifferentiated.

The modern separation of state and religion—that is at the core of American political self-description and (if not to an even higher degree) characterizes contemporary developments in Europe and other parts of the world—went along with a separation of law and religion. From time to time U.S. judges may try to preserve the presence of Christian symbols in their courthouses, but this is not a generally accepted practice. The law is supposed to be religiously neutral and, given the multireligious societies that are now so prevalent in a globalized world, it is explicitly not faith-based in many countries. While religion and the law certainly share a common past, their separation has become a social fact around the globe. Their union is now history, a history that few want to revive. Of course, exceptions exist (for instance Afghanistan under the Taliban), but these are generally met with suspicion and tend to be seen as rather backward or even medieval.

I think that the argument from morality is a secularized version of the argument from religion. Consequently, it is a historical rather than a foundational argument. In time it will probably become as obsolete as the argument from religion is today. A decoupling of ethics and law has already followed upon the decoupling of law and religion. It looks as if this evolution of the law toward more and more religious as well as moral autonomy is to continue and intensify.

Certainly there were, and still are, cases in which the term "justice" had, at the same time and indistinguishably, a religious, ethical, and legal meaning. Nowadays these meanings have become increasingly distinct. Only a few people in Western countries identify legal justice with divine justice. Fewer and fewer people, I dare to speculate, identify ethical justice with legal justice. And I don't see this cynically as an effect of crafty and immoral lawyers, but, on the contrary, the evolution of an amoral legal system. In the course of the secularization that took place during the Enlightenment, there was a transition from a religious to an ethical understanding of justice. In our times of an increasingly functionally differentiated society there is a transition from an ethical to a legal understanding of justice. Justice is now more and more accepted as a legal value that is produced within the legal system. It no longer needs direct input from priests or from ethics professors to identify what is just (or, rather, what is legal). A judge is no longer necessarily expected to know what is religiously or morally just, but what is and is not in accordance with the law. Just as no judge in Europe or North America is supposed to judge a case on the basis of her interpretation of the Bible, the Torah, or the Koran, no judge is expected to decide a case on the basis of her interpretation of Kant, Bentham, Habermas, or Rawls. In fact, religious practice, regardless of the type, is not a qualification for becoming a judge. Similarly, one does not become a judge on the basis of one's familiarity with the categorical imperative. Again, this is not to say that neither the Bible nor Kant had any influence on the history of law, but this influence is *historical*. Legal practice in Europe and North America (as well as in many other regions in the world) normally does not come to decisions on the basis of religious scriptures or through consultation with theological experts, nor does it do so by studying the classics of moral philosophy and consulting with their professional interpreters. And I think that this is, in a practical sense, good. I would want to be tried neither by a religious tribunal nor by a committee of Kantians. Legal decisions are now usually arrived at by looking at other legal decisions and texts that were produced in the legal system itself. The legal system has developed the ability to identify what is just and legal. It no longer relies on religious or moral scriptures, but can distinguish between legal and illegal on its own terms.

Within the legal system there are a number of system-internal distinctions made with respect to the act of killing: homicides of various degrees, manslaughter, different kinds of carelessness leading to the death of others, and so on. None of these distinctions is primarily religious or moral. Someone who commits manslaughter is not deemed less evil than a murderer by a court, but guilty of a lesser crime. Even if people often talk metaphorically about crimes that are more or less evil, the law cannot really measure such moral quality. There is a hierarchy of severity with respect to crimes, and the legal system has to decide in every case about the legal and not the moral categorization of a crime.

Another, and perhaps better, example is stealing. Hegel criticized Kant and the notion of the categorical imperative with reference to stealing, and I referred to this criticism in chapter 6. Here I look at it from a slightly different perspective. According to Kant, stealing is, on principle, immoral because no one can wish that the right to steal should become a universal law. Hegel, however, points out, that the very notion of stealing depends on the contingent definition of what constitutes property.[2] Only property can be stolen, but what is property? Is property limited to goods, or can, for instance, land also be considered property? How about other resources such as water and air? How about intellectual property? Or private property in general? Is private property on principle more or less moral than public property? Is nationalization stealing from individuals; is privatization stealing from the public? Can taxes be considered as stealing money from individuals? Is tax evasion stealing from the public? All of these questions depend on socially and historically contingent legal evaluations. There is no universal principle that can define the nature of property and, consequently, the moral and legal characterization of stealing. What is legally considered to be stealing cannot be derived from any moral principles. The law has to distance itself from utopian moral categorical imperatives in order to be able to deal with these cases. It has to build up internal complexity, for example by constructing a very complex range of definitions of property and stealing, in order to be able to deal with such issues in contemporary society. A law that would deal with these situations in a Kantian manner would function poorly and primitively. It would not be able to do justice—in a legal and not moral sense—to the complex problems regarding ownership in today's society.

This means, of course, as well that what is legal or legally just is not necessarily religiously or morally just. Again, I think that this is much preferable to a situation in which religious, moral, and legal justice are congruent. The diversification of justice is socially beneficial since it allows for much greater complexity than a single transcendent justice. I think it is as impossible to characterize the justice that is produced in the legal system in terms of any religion as it is in terms of any moral philosophy or specific set of moral values. Simply put, the speed limit or the legal amount of alcohol present in the blood can neither be deduced from the Bible nor from Kant. Trying to do this would be absurd.

In our society, the law is no longer influenced primarily by religious or moral beliefs. It exists within the highly complex environment of a number of other systems, including the economy, politics, mass media, medicine, education, and science. None of these systems functions in a specific moral or ethical manner. All of them, however, factually exert great influence on the law and vice versa. The law has to consider—in its own terms—what goes on in all of these other systems. Just as it has to deal with issues concerning property (in the economy), it has to deal with the contingency and complexity of what goes on in other systems. It has to define laws for election processes, for the media, for medicine, and so on. Is, for instance, an election format based on proportional representation more moral than one that is not? Are elections in the United States more or less good than those in Germany? None of these questions can be reduced to ethical categories alone.

On the one hand, the legal system has to deal with the social systems in its environment. On the other hand, the other systems are also more or less dependent on the law for their own functioning. And again, this is not a moral issue. Politicians, for instance, rely on the law to define the right election process so that an election can actually be held regardless of its assumed moral character. Many of those who think that a mixed membership parliament would be more just still vote in Canada, even though such a system is not in place. Corporations normally obey legal decisions, even if they find them unfair. Every other system profits from the clarity of legal decisions—and from their changeability. Systems would overburden themselves if they had to constantly question the moral validity of their rules. They simply follow the law—and try to change it if they want.

There is a case that illustrates the demoralization of law quite nicely. When I was a teenager in Germany in the 1970s I liked to watch a TV show called *Marriages at Court* (*Ehen vor Gericht*). It was a "serious" documentation of real divorce cases that was very different in character from the current *Judge So-and-So* shows. It consisted of reenactments of court scenes and legal commentaries and analyses. The show was interesting because of what German law was like at the time. In a divorce, the court had to determine which of the spouses was "guilty" (for instance, because of cheating). The one who was found guilty usually could not claim much financial support, so there was a lot at stake. (I remember noticing at some point that I always sympathized with the man and never with the woman, regardless of who had been the cheater. I also remember listening with fascination to my parents and relatives gossiping about divorcees in our town and saying things like: "She is divorced—and she was found guilty!" At that time there was still a significant social stigma attached to being divorced, not to mention being the guilty one.) The show came to an end when German divorce law was radically reformed. It seems, due in no small measure to feminist efforts, that the old laws were found to be highly problematic and often unjust, particularly given the social reality at that time when married women tended to give up their careers and thus became economically dependent on their husbands. If a wife was found guilty this could easily mean financial ruin and the loss of her children, since she would not be able to support them.

But the main problem with the old law was not so much its (perhaps unintended) unfairness to women, but the fact that naming one of the parties guilty is not so much a legal as a *moral* decision. Cheating is not really a crime if one looks at it from a nonreligious and amoral perspective. Cheating (not to speak of other supposed spousal shortcomings that were pointed out in various cases by the competing lawyers) may be a sin or evil, but it is very hard to identify it as illegal on the basis of contemporary law. It became harder and harder to provide legal criteria for proving the guilt of one spouse and the innocence of the other. This is often quite easy when moral or religious judgments are applied, but what constitutes guilt and innocence in a very complex intimate relationship? The law came to understand that it was dealing here with matters that were simply outside its purview. The German reform of the divorce law then abolished the guilty/innocent distinction altogether so that the courts now regulate financial and childcare matters without recourse to these categories. (They do, of course, have to take the *illegal* actions of a spouse into account, such as the use of physical violence.)

I think the reform of German divorce law shows very clearly how the legal system has decoupled itself not only from religious creeds but also from moral evaluations. Moral judgments or values do not parallel legal criteria and they can easily become an obstacle within legal procedures. The old German divorce law overburdened the judges with moral questions and led the lawyers of the opposing spouses to introduce moral accusations into their arguments. The new law acknowledged the fact that the legal system had decoupled itself from moral discourses and had to apply its own criteria rather than rely on vague considerations about what was morally decent. I, for one, am quite happy to live in a society where one spouse cannot bring the other to court for cheating. (In the United States, one has the equally unappealing possibility of going on a TV show like

Jerry Springer or *Cheaters*, but this is an issue for the chapter on morality and the mass media.)

In order to clarify what I mean by the separation of law and morality, I present a parallel example, namely the separation of rules and morality in sports. In sports, the equivalent of justice is "fairness."[3] And I think that just as legal justice should not be equated with moral justice, fairness in sports is not to be equated with moral fairness. The fairness of sports rules differ very much from, for instance, ethical fairness as defined by John Rawls. Rawls' model is, simply put, based on the hypothetical idea that fairness is constituted by the agreement or consensus that would be reached by all members of a society or community regardless of their actual status within this community (that is under the condition of the famous "veil of ignorance"). It would then, according to Rawls, be in everybody's interest to agree on rules that would be acceptable for them independent of their role in society. They would necessarily have to agree to rules that would be fair to all members of society, because if the rules were not fair in this sense, everyone would run the risk of ending up in a social position (a woman, a handicapped person, etc.) that would be subject to unfair treatment. Rawls' idea of fairness is to a certain degree quite Kantian in that it presupposes some transcendental or a priori status of fairness. Rawls' hypothetical fairness precedes social practice. It is grounded in some sort of (hypothetical) fundamental consensus that is both prelegal and extralegal. Concrete laws would have to be constructed according to principles that are not ultimately derived from the legal system itself but from Rawls' philosophical definition of "fairness." In order to be fair, laws and other rules must correspond with the ethical principle identified by the ethicist. The standard for what is legally fair, or, in other words, just, is thus not a legal but an ethical standard that is more fundamental than law itself. I think that neither legal fairness (i.e., justice) nor fairness in sports functions in a Rawlsian way in our society. And I think it should not function in such a way. Or in Wittgensteinian terms: If we use the word "fair" in everyday language, we do not mean an a priori fairness. We use it in a relative sense. By calling something fair, we normally think that it is not absolutely fair but fair enough.

I use the example of basketball to illustrate my point. Most people would agree that the rules of basketball are reasonably fair. In fact, everyone who competes in this sport, to a certain extent, implicitly accepts the fairness of the rules. Obviously, if a player did not think the rules were fair and refused, for instance, to accept a penalty for a foul or some other violation of the rules, she would not play the game for long. However, it would be absurd to state that the rules of basketball are fair in Rawls' sense. Obviously, given the veil of ignorance, people would probably have a major problem with the height of the baskets, since it gives an unfair advantage to the very tall. Most are not fairly treated by the standardized height. It would be much fairer, in a Rawlsian sense, to calculate the height of the baskets on the basis of the average height of the players on all the teams.

Virtually every sport includes rules that are fundamentally unfair in the Rawlsian sense. Some give advantages to the tall, some to the fast, and others to the strong. In fact, I think it would be rather difficult to identify a single rule in sports that is fair in accordance with the veil of ignorance. Nevertheless fairness remains a widely acknowledged principle in competitive sports. It is clear that fairness functions well enough without being justified on the basis of ethical principles. To state that those rules that are accepted as fair in sports must be derived from ethical deliberations would be absurd. Of course, as I say throughout this book, I do not mean that the rules in sports are unethical or immoral, only that they are nonethical or amoral, and that this is precisely why they function well. I do not think that sports could ever work on the basis of a foundationally ethical principle of fairness as the one suggested by Rawls (or any other moral philosopher). The notion of fairness in sports is developed within the system of sports. It is the system of sports itself that has produced its own standards of fairness, which have no direct or causal relation to any specific set of moral principles. They cannot be derived from Rawls, Kant, Bentham, or Habermas. This makes them very dynamic: They can evolve, they can change, and yet they are still stable in the sense that most people who are affected by them accept them rather happily. Nobody who plays basketball has to care about the congruence of the rules with any given moral or religious doctrine. And I think that this makes playing and watching basketball a lot more fun than if it were otherwise.

Niklas Luhmann has, in his characteristically reader-unfriendly manner, coined the concept of a contingency formula to explain the function of the notion of justice in the legal system. In exactly the same sense, I suggest, fairness can be called the contingency formula in sports. A contingency formula is a rather paradoxical thing. It is necessarily contingent; that is, it is subject to constant change and not based on any determining principles. No one can ultimately define what is "just" in the legal system or "fair" in sports. This is decided within the respective systems, in terms of the specific system, and these decisions change from day to day. What is legal today can easily be illegal tomorrow and obviously the same is true for what is considered fair in sports. Despite (or, paradoxically, exactly because of) the contingent nature of a contingency formula, it serves the function of making "something that is seen as highly artificial and contingent from the outside appear quite natural and necessary from the inside." In the legal system, justice is taken for granted as that which all legal procedures aim to establish: "The system itself has to define justice in such a way that makes it clear that justice must prevail and that the system identifies with it as an idea, principle, or value. The formula for contingency is stated within the system non-contentiously."[4]

From the outside, the philosophical observer can see that neither legal justice nor fairness in sports is derived from any noncontingent (moral) principles. At the same time, one can also observe that the contingency formulas as such are (normally) not contested within the systems. What is specifically deemed just or fair constantly changes, but this by no means diminishes the acceptance of justice or fairness as the idea behind the specific rules defined within the systems. A new law or a new rule in basketball is soon accepted as just or fair, sometimes even more so than the previous one. The contingency of the specific rules does not lead to mistrust in the justice or fairness within the systems; on the contrary, it allows for the stability of the formulas. It is the flexibility, and particularly, I would say, the *amoral* flexibility, of the contingency formulas that makes them so durable. Luhmann says, with respect to the legal system, that justice "is not adduced in its function as a formula for contingency but as a value."[5] The same is true for fairness in sports. And it is precisely the blindness for the contingency of the contingency formula and its acceptance as a noncontentious value within the system that makes it work so well. It seems, paradoxically, that it is good for athletes and judges to counterfactually believe that they act in accordance with (moral or other) values since this allows for the amoral functioning of the respective systems.

My argument for the separation of morality and law is based on the idea that the legal system is now autonomous enough to produce both the distinction between what is legal and illegal and thus the contingency formula of justice out of its own communications processes. The idea of the increasing autonomy of the law, of its capability of differing out, of distinguishing itself from other social systems, should not be mistaken as ascribing to the legal system the ability to produce its own legal (if not moral) universal principles. Some authors suggest that the legal system has become powerful enough to establish its own code (legal/illegal) within society without having to rely on other systems or its environment (moral discourse, for instance) to provide it with foundational principles. Often, however, people who suppose such an autonomy say that instead of borrowing foundational principles from the outside, the law produces (or, at least, could produce) its own foundational principles. This means, of course, that while accepting the autonomy of the legal system, one nevertheless denies the idea that justice is a contingency formula. Certain foundational rights identified within the legal system would then be just as much foundational principles as the old religious or ethical principles. These principles would be legal principles, but that makes them in no way more contingent than, let's say, the categorical imperative or the Ten Commandments. Religious and ethical principles are thus substituted by legal principles that are also seen as universally valid. Such an argument can be heard quite frequently with respect to human rights. Human rights are often described as inalienable and immediately related to the dignity of the human being as such. In this view, such rights are believed to be legal principles that, once formulated, will serve as the foundation of justice within the legal system.

One major representative of such a view on human rights is, in my reading, Martha Nussbaum. Nussbaum looks at human rights from a feminist perspective and believes that the law, and particularly human rights law, is the most important tool to bring about equality among the sexes and to diminish the suffering of women around the world. In one particularly interesting book she discusses the not so uncommon conflicts between religious discourses or practices and women's rights.[6] There have existed and there continue to exist a number of religious discourses that justify the physical mutilation of the female body and even the killing of women under specific circumstances (once more, one may think of Afghanistan under the Taliban). Obviously, a dilemma arises in such cases: If one approves of such practices on the basis of the right for the freedom of religion then one will at the same time compromise what Nussbaum calls the "basic human rights" of individuals. There are situations in which a group's claim to religious freedom may entail violations of human rights, and if this happens, Nussbaum argues, precedence must be given to individual human rights because they are the more fundamental principle. She states: "A human right, unlike many other rights people may have, derives not from a person's particular situation or privilege or power or skill, but, instead, just from the fact of being human."[7]

I think that such a claim is highly problematic. I am not arguing in favor of the mutilation and killing of women (or any other human being), but I do not see how such deeds can be (legally) condemned "just from the fact of being human." From the standpoint of the moral fool, I do not see how human nature disallows killing, mutilation, or any other cruel act. Would it not be equally possible to say that human rights, if derived solely from what it means to be human, should allow for killing and mutilation because, as an empirical fact, that's what human beings have always done. These acts seem to be an integral part of human nature—if one believes in the existence of such a thing. I think it is impossible to derive any legal principle merely from the fact of being human. Who decides which legal decisions necessarily follow from this fact? Martha Nussbaum or Osama bin Laden? How can one claim to know precisely which human rights are to be inferred from this fact? I am afraid that a position like Nussbaum's can easily lead to a legal fundamentalism or to a "human rights fundamentalism" to use a term coined by Niklas Luhmann.[8] It makes no particular difference if one transforms religious or ethical claims into legal claims, if one declares such legal claims to be as universally valid as the former. War can be justified as easily on the basis of the principles of human rights as on the basis of inalienable religious or moral values. What makes these principles dangerous is the very fact that they may be declared to be universally valid or fundamental. If the contingency of such contingency formulas as justice, fairness, or faith is fundamentally denied, then social conflict looms. A certain blindness is needed with respect to the contingency of justice of the legal system. If one has a role within the legal system, it is useful not to constantly question the value of justice and just suppose that the system somehow operates justly. It is counterproductive, though, if this unquestioning belief in the justice of the legal system is radicalized into a legal fundamentalism. If certain rights are declared to be fundamental or unassailable, then the contingency of the contingency formula is endangered and this, in turn, can easily lead to a loss of flexibility in the system—which makes it more prone to failure.

Here I side with pragmatists like Richard Rorty in opposing the attempts of human rights fundamentalists to define what is just, right, and legal on the basis of supposedly universal principles (as derived from such problematic notions as human nature) regardless of whether these principles are labeled religious, moral, or legal. Rorty supports the idea that the purported ability to fundamentally justify human rights has become obsolete and meaningless.[9] In fact, we do not need any notion of human nature in order to legally condemn such acts as murder or genocide. The legal system does not have to rely on a specific definition of the human in order to distinguish between what it deems legal and illegal. It is current legal practice to call genocide a war crime and to prosecute people who are guilty of it. Just as with justice, it may not be a problem if people believe that this happens on the basis of human rights as long as they do not actually claim to have a fundamental definition and universal understanding of what these rights are. It seems to Rorty (and to me) that any foundational claim within legal discourse is not only unhelpful for coming up with a functional legal system, but may in fact be obstructive, even dangerous. If justice and human rights are tacitly (or, as one can say in German *stillschweigend*, i.e., "without thematizing it explicitly in the system") accepted as a contingency formula, then the system seems to be running in a safer manner than when this is not the case.

The decoupling of the law, its separation from morality, is an effect of its ability to establish itself as an autopoietic, self-constituting system. I cannot see any empirical evidence why this decoupling from morality should be more problematic or more harmful than the identification of religious, moral, and legal values in the past. In fact, so far the separation of morality and law seems to have worked out quite well for most of those involved.

9 | MORALITY AND CIVIL RIGHTS

I AM GRATEFUL TO Franklin Perkins for coming up with another important challenge to my defense of amorality in connection with the issue of ethics and law. Frank acknowledges that ethical discourse can be dangerous and often quite appalling, for instance with respect to such cases as the war in Iraq, the Lewinsky scandal, or the murder of doctors who perform abortions. But he says that there are also ethical discourses that are very beneficial, such as those of civil rights movements. He suggests that the benefits of ethical discourse and moral appeals might well outweigh the dangers of the abuses of ethics. I comment on the problematic notion of abuse in the introduction, so I won't repeat myself here. I will, however, discuss the issue of ethics and civil rights in this chapter in more detail. There is a great deal of merit to Frank's position and it must be addressed.

My response to Frank's challenge is very much in line with the argument that I presented in the preceding chapter. I think that the idea that ethics were an important aspect of civil rights movements is probably historically correct, but society has evolved in such a way that ethics are no longer needed to fight for rights. On the contrary, I think that civil rights movements have moved beyond ethical positions and have, to a large extent, separated morality and law. These movements have benefited from this separation and have become more successful because of it. The very term "civil rights movements" gives us a clue: Civil rights movements are not called "civil ethics movements"; they focus on *rights*, not on morality.

Following Niklas Luhmann, I believe that "functional differentiation" is the most important structural characteristic of contemporary society. In our globalized world, society is no longer *primarily* divided according to geographical or class differences (although these differences obviously still exist) but into different function systems. For the most part, what we *are* socially is determined by the roles we play within these function systems: We may be students in the education system, patients in the medical system, husbands at home, the opposition in parliament, a defendant at court, or a customer in a shop. How we communicate (what we actually say, how we behave socially) is determined not so much by where we live or by the family that we were born into but by the various function systems we are in at any given time. At the university, for instance, we communicate according to the communicational forms that were developed in the systems of education and science. We write exams, assign marks, write academic papers, counsel students, and write letters of reference. At court, we have to communicate in the way that one communicates within the legal system. If we do not, we are not taken seriously in the system. We are not supposed to express our love, bargain about a fine, or give a political speech in the courtroom. Under different forms of social differentiation, our family status or place of birth may well have been more important in court than any other criteria. Nowadays such things still matter, but one can only communicate effectively if one does so according to the communicative patterns of the various social function systems. In this way, functional differentiation structures contemporary society.

It does not seem to be the case that there is such thing as a moral system, that is, a specific function system comparable to education, politics, the economy, or the legal system. Obviously, moral communication can be used—and is used—in all systems from time to time (politicians especially tend to do so), but no system operates on the basis of the code good/evil. With respect to the legal system, for instance, the code legal/illegal is not primarily a moral distinction but a legal one.

Civil rights movements are also subject to functional differentiation, and they seem to have evolved historically in a fashion that allows them to operate quite effectively under the conditions of this social structure. They have understood that in order to reach their goals they cannot simply demand moral recognition (once more: there is no moral system in society) but must strive for certain rights in the legal system, certain political powers, and access to institutions in the education or medical system. Historically, civil rights movements may have focused on moral recognition, but it has become quite obvious that the demand for such recognition, some sort of a social consensus that it is not evil to be black or gay, for instance, does not get blacks or gays very far in society. Legal rights, political powers, and access to education are much more important for these groups than moral acceptance. It seems to me that African Americans, gays and lesbians, women, and immigrants are no longer very interested in moral recognition. Many homosexuals and African Americans, for example, think that they should be treated not morally, but amorally. They are not so concerned about how moral others think they are as whether they have the same rights as other people.

In fact it is not only more important but also more realistic to claim certain rights, powers, and access to institutions than moral recognition. How do you make everyone think that gays or African Americans are morally good? This would be quite a difficult thing to do. It is comparatively easier, and more in line with functional differentiation, to grant voting rights to women, legalize gay marriage, and accept African Americans at universities. Struggles for such civil rights have proven to be quite effective because they operate in line with existing social structures. Moral struggles are more difficult to fight and are not so likely to bring about any concrete social results. Perhaps it was historically useful for civil rights movements to begin their struggles with ethical communication, but in order for them to be successful in contemporary society they had to go beyond morality. They had to adjust to the existing separation between morality and law (and the other function systems).

Civil rights movements for women, African Americans, and gays have been relatively successful. Of course, they did not bring about total equality, but a good number of their demands have been met. Women can vote in most countries; African Americans can go to any university in the United States; and gays can marry in Canada. I think that there is a significant difference between civil rights movements and protests such as antiwar, antiglobalization, and environmental movements. The difference is, I believe, that, for various reasons, protest movements are not as advanced. They are not as successful as civil rights movements because they have not yet been able to switch from primarily moral discourse to, for instance, legal discourse.

Antiwar movements such as those against the conflicts in Vietnam and Iraq have been dominated by ethical arguments. Most protesters considered the wars to be immoral. This, of course, reflects the moral argumentation of political leaders. Nixon could not end the Vietnam war as soon as he might have wished because he aimed at a peace with honor. Tony Blair pointed out again and again the moral necessity of the war against an evil regime in Iraq. While many protesters point out that the second Gulf War is not only immoral, but also illegal, this argument does not, in my view, get the same attention or emphasis as the argument from morality. There have been no specific demands for changes in the law, at least none that I am aware of. This is, I think, quite different from the civil rights movements discussed above. I am not suggesting, however, that the antiwar movements should be blamed for their relative inefficiency and backwardness. They cannot demand legal changes because war is not a legal matter to begin with. The problem with wars is that they are too loosely coupled to, for instance, the legal system. The legal system has not really developed the capacity to effectively irritate wars. There are laws in place that deal with armed conflicts but they do not have much influence on actual wars. Military and political leaders are able to make their decisions without having to worry much about legal consequences. Wars seem to have a closer coupling with the economy and the mass media. The U.S. military and government are more worried about media coverage of war than about any legal resonance. War can be waged without legal or political consent (at the UN) but it cannot be fought without a certain support from the media, particularly in North America. The success or failure of a conflict seems to be more closely related to the mass media than to the legal system. (This is an issue that I discuss in chapters 11 and 12.)

The antiglobalization and the environmental movement share the moralist inclinations of antiwar movements. They too have not yet matured. The demands, at least those that are made known, of the antiglobalization movement are not specific: It is against capitalism and multinational corporations, and it is for the poor and a world that is fairer and more just. There may well be a number of legal and other functional demands but these seem to be overshadowed by a general moralist rhetoric. The ethical appeal of such words as "fair" and "just" seems to be too strong for this movement to actually focus on demands that can be fulfilled by society.

The environmental movement has made a lot of progress toward becoming as effective as certain civil rights movements. Concrete legal, political, and economic demands are increasingly made. There are calls for political treaties and a regulation of emission standards. Some countries have introduced tax penalties for pollution. Still, the label "green" is quite diffuse and often represents not much more than the moral self-accusation of society: We have spoiled the earth for our children; we are living an excessive life; we have lost touch with nature; we need to change our environmental consciousness; would Jesus drive an SUV? Such ethical appeals are rather widespread among environmentalists. Within this movement there remains an obsession with environmental ethics that distracts it from more functional demands.

I stress that I do not think of any of the above movements as morally right or wrong. I do not know and am not interested in the question of whether the war in Iraq is ethically justified or not. It is not helpful to discuss war in ethical terms. However, I think that it was illegal to begin with. I also do not care much about the ethics of women's rights. I cannot vote in national elections in the country I live in (because I am not an Irish citizen), and I do not care. I do not find this unethical or unfair. I am not sure if voting is a human right. It is legal for women to vote in Ireland and this obviously contributes to the stability of the political system and society as a whole. Here it would be absolutely unjust, in a legal sense, to deny a woman the right to vote—except if she were under eighteen years old, in which case her vote would be illegal. I do not know how to ethically justify why a seventeen-year-old cannot vote (or that a citizen can, and a permanent resident cannot), but this is the law and both the legal and political systems function quite well in this way. I do not think that issues about war, voting rights, the treatment of

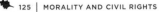

ethnic or sexual minorities, or the environment are fundamentally moral issues nor do I think that an ethical approach is very effective in dealing with them. It is my opinion that women should have a legal right to an abortion, but this opinion does not follow from any ethical principle. I am too much of a moral fool to say if women have the moral right to do so and if this legal right can therefore be deducted from an ethical principle. I would not take part in a debate about the ethical justification of abortion but I would defend this right legally.

I think it is only fair enough (just as I think that basketball rules are fair enough) for women to have certain rights with respect to their bodies. In most but not all countries in which the legal system operates autopoietically, abortion has been legalized under various conditions and often in response to demands for women's rights. In countries with drastic antiabortion laws (Poland, for instance), the legal system seems to be highly sensitive to irritations from religion, which, in turn, appears to diminish the potential for certain civil rights movements (women, gays, etc.) to be successful.

When the legal system is very tightly coupled with other systems (such as the religious system, but one may also think of political or economic systems),civil rights movements seem to face greater difficulties. Just as moral discourse and moral arguments may in some cases help civil rights movements, it is equally possible (and perhaps even more likely) that the influence of moral discourse on the legal system can act as an obstacle. It simply depends on where the moral majority lies—and typically civil rights movements represent minority claims. In many U.S. states people hold religious and other beliefs that make gay marriage appear immoral to them. Since in some of these states the law lacks autonomy, civil rights initiatives to legalize gay marriage are unsuccessful. So far, every single U.S. state that has had a referendum on gay marriage has denied this right. The right has only been granted where legal institutions are autonomous enough to come to legal decisions independently of the moral majority. I think it is quite obvious that there is no correlation between the success of civil rights movements and the use of moral discourse. It can be, has been, and still is as useful in arguing for certain civil rights as it is for arguing against them. In some cases civil rights movements have profited from moral arguments; in other cases the opposite is the case. In every case, however, such movements profit more from and aim more at certain legal rights than moral recognition. Of course, the granting of legal rights may also lead to greater moral acceptance of certain groups, but if this is the case, this only demonstrates once more that these groups seem to fare better if they focus primarily on the law rather than on ethics.

I support my hypothesis that moral discourse, indeed ethics in general, is a very dubious and uncertain ally of human rights movements by taking a closer look at what is probably its most crucial historical predecessor in North America, namely the abolitionist movement of the nineteenth century—and at its peculiar sister, the prohibition movement.

To begin with, I point out what, in my view, is the most important difference between these historical movements and more current civil rights movements. Abolitionism and prohibition were mainly movements *against* something; they focused on abolishing and prohibiting widespread practices whereas today's movements are largely movements *for* something. I know, of course, that every against corresponds to a for (to be against slavery is to be for freedom, to be against drinking is to be for temperance), but I think that the emphasis here is important, and the self-designations of those groups were very explicit about where this emphasis lay. The abolitionists and the prohibitionists wanted laws that forbade something, whereas most contemporary civil rights movements focus on demanding new rights—and even those that want to abolish certain rights today, such as the antiabortionists, prefer to give themselves a positive designation, such as pro-life.

It is also significant, I believe, that both the abolitionist and the prohibitionist movements were largely *white* movements and were deeply rooted in various versions of religious (mainly Protestant) fundamentalism. They both relied on religious and moral arguments to make legal demands, and these demands, I dare say, were largely made by whites and were directed primarily at fellow whites. These circumstances are particularly interesting with respect to abolitionism. If my understanding of the history of abolitionism is correct, it consisted mainly of certain whites demanding of other whites not to do something (possessing slaves) because of its immoral and religiously reprehensible character and, accordingly, to outlaw this practice. (The same could clearly be said about prohibition.) Abolitionism's first aim was to abolish the practice of having slaves and the right to have slaves. It seems that considerations about the positive side of the claim—granting equal rights to African Americans, and so on—were only, and at most, of secondary relevance. Yes, there was a lot of talk about the terrible fate of the slaves and the need to set them free, but this was mainly directed at the slave owners. This moral rhetoric focused more on making those involved with slavery feel guilty than on pointing out that blacks deserved the same rights as whites. In this sense, abolitionism was only secondarily, if at all, an antiracist movement; it was much more a moral and religious movement against sinners. (And, once more, the same is true for prohibition.)

While most historians agree that slavery was only one among many issues that led to the American Civil War, it was certainly the most morally and religiously charged issue. It allowed the North to claim moral and religious superiority over the South. The (white) Southerners were accused of being evil sinners who should thus be deprived of a right that many of them felt was essential to their livelihood and social status. The Southerners were equally sure that they had God and morality on their side. In 1832 Thomas Roderick Dew, professor of history, metaphysics, and political law at William and Mary stated: "Slavery was established and sanctioned by divine authority, among even the elect of heaven, the favored children of Israel. Abraham, the founder of this interesting nation, and the chosen servant of the Lord, was the owner of *hundreds* of slaves."[1]

The Civil War broke out as a war of secession, and one of the main reasons for this was that Southerners did not want to give up their peculiar institution and be deprived of their slave-owning privileges. On both sides, the abolition of rights and practices, not the granting of rights and practices, was the primary concern and thus the conflict over abolition was not so much about the civil rights of blacks as about the moral and religious (and thus legal and economic) differences between whites.

From today's perspective no one denies that the abolition of slavery was a good thing and that through the victory of the North, African Americans were granted a most important human right, namely the right to liberty. In this way, one can indeed say that the moral and religious discourse involved in the conflict helped bring about specific legal progress. (Of course, things would have been different, but certainly no less morally and religiously acclaimed, if the South had won.) Even given the strong emphasis on moral and religious issues (by the whites), legal progress did not go much further than the mere abolition of slavery. Once the sinners (the Southerners) were deprived of their rights, once *white* America had morally and religiously purged itself, few positive legal measures (for the blacks) were deemed necessary. Yes, there was freedom, but not much more. Because the struggle for abolition was (largely) a moral and religious struggle between whites, and only secondarily a legal struggle for the rights of blacks, it led to not much more than the legal elimination of slavery. Abolitionism was more successful and legally influential than prohibition, but both movements were, I believe, based on moral and religious discourse and could therefore not really initiate justice. (I use this term here, of course, in the sense of a contingency formula.) Abolitionism identified and finally led to the abolishment of an injustice, but it did not do much to set up just legal standards.

It took the (largely) black civil rights movement of the twentieth century to actually improve the *positive* legal status of African Americans. As is unavoidable in a highly moral and religious society like the United States, the civil rights movement of the 1950s and '60s certainly made ample use of moral and religious discourse, but an emphasis on legal issues was more prevalent. The movement was concerned with specific rights such as access to public transportation and lunch counters, schools and universities, careers and political power. This civil rights movement was not fueled by whites' wishes for moral and religious self-purification but by blacks' interests in rights they believed they justly deserved.

While I think that the comparison between the abolitionist movement in the nineteenth century and the (ongoing) African American civil rights movement of the twentieth century shows that morality (and religion) may contribute to or even initiate, to a certain extent, legal reform and change, civil right movements clearly have to leave moral and religious reasoning largely behind in order to realize their legal goals under current social conditions. Ethical communication may help civil rights causes at times, but it can equally well be used against them. It seems to me that African Americans are now much more interested in issues related to social function systems such as the law, the economy, politics, education, and the medical system than with merely ideal, or rather semantic or rhetorical, issues such as morality. If the African American civil rights movement was able to go beyond abolitionism, it is because the former is less ethical than its predecessor.

10 | HOW TO GET A DEATH VERDICT

I AM NOT OPPOSED to the death penalty on principle, and I am certainly not opposed to it because of fundamental moral (or religious) convictions—since I lack these. I believe that historically the death penalty served certain social purposes. Earlier societies had, for various reasons, not been able to establish a legal system that could deal with crime in a complex fashion and often could not establish the institution of the prison as a major agency of punishment. Such societies (ancient China, for instance) relied mainly on corporal punishment, including beatings, mutilation, torture, and executions. I am certainly happy to live in a society where I will most likely never be exposed to such modes of punishment. But given historical and social contingencies, I find it hard to condemn such civilizations as inherently or principally immoral.

In some circumstances I think that what could be called extralegal death sentences are socially appropriate even today. Given the conditions of the revolution in Romania in 1989, the execution of the Ceauşescus, which did not result from due legal process,[1] seems to have been the right (socially and politically, but not necessarily legally or morally) thing to do. Had the military coup to assassinate Hitler succeeded, my home country would most likely have been spared from much of its devastation—and the concentration camps might well have closed earlier. I also did not grieve when I heard that fellow inmates had killed Jeffrey Dahmer in prison. It is hard to always remain the moral fool. Still, I think that the legal system should, as much as possible, avoid moral sentiment and extralegal killing. The legal system works best when it tends toward moral foolishness.

I strongly argue against the death penalty in this chapter, but not for moral reasons and not on principle. Instead, I try to make an amoral and antimoral case against the specific pseudolegal practice of the death penalty in the United States today.[2] In fact, I try to show that morality is to blame for both the ideological and philosophical justification of this anachronistic practice as well as for the many legal problems associated with it, such as, in particular, the staggering extent of wrongful convictions. I do not, and this has to be stressed, think that the current moral (and religious) condemnation of the death penalty in the United States is appropriate nor do I think it will be effective in abolishing the death penalty. Morality is not the solution to this pseudolegal practice of the death penalty, but, on the contrary, is itself at the heart of the problem.

Continuing my argumentation of the two preceding chapters, I give a concrete example of the damage that is done when morality is imposed on the legal system, when it becomes, so to speak, morally infected, and thus loses its operational autonomy. Put very concretely: I hope to show through the example of death penalty practice in the United States what happens when offenders are conceived of as evil more than as criminals. I hope to show what happens when legal justice is twisted into moral justice.

It is interesting to look at the recent history of the death penalty on an international scale. In 1985, the large majority of all countries, 130 out of 176, were retentionist, that is, they practiced the death penalty. The percentage then declined steeply. A mere sixteen years later, only 86 out of 195 countries were still retentionist.[3] I do not think the main reason for this development is an increase in global morality, or an understanding of the universal validity of supposed human rights. After all, most countries that *do* have the death penalty (including the United States) present themselves as highly respectful of either human rights or moral principles (Iran)—and, as I show, sometimes even point out that the death penalty is a human right![4] Instead, I think the demise of the death penalty can be described as an effect of the emancipation of the legal system from moral, political, and religious domination. The above statistics strongly suggest that along with the currently increasing functional differentiation of the legal system, the death penalty is more and more regarded as an illegal form of punishment. Just as other function systems no longer equate their value distinction with moral distinctions, the legal system has to a large extent separated itself from moral discourse. The result of this is clear: When bad students or opposition politicians are not regarded as evil, and instead are seen as being underperformers or losers in an election, they may get bad grades or less powerful positions but they are not beaten or killed—they are not exposed to personal and thus often corporal sanctions. Moral judgments aim at the whole person, including her bodily existence—and thus the whole person, including her body, may become the object of sanctions. If a bad student is seen as personally guilty of his bad performance then it makes perfect sense to beat him. If an opposition politician is seen as evil (or as rebellious) then it seems only right to get rid of him.[5] Corporal punishment makes sense because a person is not seen as merely a bad student or a bad politician but as fundamentally flawed and wicked. If, however, a system ignores those aspects of an individual's existence (the body of the person, for instance) that are irrelevant for the function of the system, then it is more likely to develop its own less personal, less moral, and less corporal, but much more functional sanctions—it awards bad grades but goes no further. Marks are systemic constructs that do not relate to the whole person, but only to the person as a student. From a functional perspective a bad student is simply a bad student. From a moral perspective, a bad student is a bad person that has vices (perhaps laziness, obstinacy, an undisciplined nature). When students are morally rather than functionally evaluated, then corporal punishment is certainly an option that makes sense. Students were typically subject to corporal punishment in earlier societies that lacked fully developed functional differentiation.

Nothing in the contemporary function systems calls for a total sanctioning of the whole person and her physical life. Function systems treat individuals as students, professors, candidates, voters, or consumers with respect to their *particular* functions; they do not tend to treat them as beings that may have to be entirely destroyed if they do something truly bad. They sanction individuals in accord with their systemic functioning (e.g., if you do a bad job, you get fired; if you run slowly, you lose the race), but not with respect to their physical existence. And they do this because the physical existence of human beings is not a relevant factor in their judgments. Of course, people have to be alive in order to be able to be a student, a consumer, or a voter, but there is no specific way in which any system can account for the bare fact of being alive, and there is no reason why it would concern itself with systemically taking away life. Function systems are simply not concerned with bare life. While legal sanctions can of course be harsh and include imprisonment for extended periods of time, and thus impose severe limitations on a person's social existence and freedom, they are in societies with highly developed functional differentiation normally not corporal and do not totally exclude a person from society. Prisoners in such societies are typically not supposed to be beaten, and they are still allowed (though often in a limited way) to watch TV, be educated, practice a religion, have personal property, receive medical attention; they even have some legal and political rights. They are still able to take part in mass media communications, the education system, religion, the economy, medicine, intimacy, and the law. Negative sanctioning by social systems can be drastic (e.g., imprisonment, being fired, not being allowed to graduate) and significantly limit one's chances for success in other social systems (if one does not get a high school degree, it is more difficult to make a lot of money), but they usually remain merely social sanctions.

Sanctions in *any* system that may ultimately exclude a person from society through execution are, in a profoundly amoral and obvious sense, cruel and unusual. On the one hand, they are unusual because they do not conform to any of the codes that social systems operate with. On the other hand, they are cruel because they are an act of sheer destructive physical violence. Perhaps it is morally right to kill people legally (as most proponents of the death penalty say). Still this does not make it less cruel. I do not know if cruelty is on principle moral or immoral, but I know that killing someone who does not want to die is cruel. Probably those who killed the Ceaușescus were doing the "right" thing, though I am sure that they acted in a cruel manner. Once more, there may well be circumstances in which it may be appropriate or, for various reason, practical, to act in a cruel and unusual way (and perhaps kill others). The U.S. Constitution, however, says that this should be avoided in the legal system.

I think that the recent decrease in the application of the death penalty can be explained in the context of increasing functional differentiation. Once criminal offenders are not convicted as evildoers, and once focus shifts to their violation of the law, then corporal punishment, in particular, its most extreme form, capital punishment, becomes more and more obsolete. Those countries in which the legal system is not free from religious, moral, or political domination (such as Iran, Afghanistan, or China) seem to tend more toward the use of corporal punishment than countries with a more secular, relatively amoral, and functionally autonomous legal system (like most European countries and Canada). The United States is a very special case in the so-called Western world. While bodily punishment is illegal for most crimes (Guantanamo seems to be an exception), the death penalty is widely practiced, and it is practiced, as I hope to show, largely for moral (and partly for religious and political) reasons. The abolishment of minor corporal punishment (in most cases) and the retention of corporal punishment in its most extreme form is, in my view, an open and crass contradiction in U.S. legal practice and is clear evidence of its archaic (or should I say primitive?) character.

If the overall decreasing number of countries practicing the death penalty is indeed an effect of increasing functional differentiation on a global scale, then this is an example of how an entirely amoral and purely structural social development can contribute to the separation of law and morality in legislative matters. The widespread abolishment of the death penalty is then not due to any moral progress of lawmakers but to social changes that have led to the demoralization of various social systems, including the law and its legislative branch.

In this chapter I discuss the judicial aspects of a still overmoralized legal system. In order to do this, I first look at the philosophical or ideological justifications of the death penalty in America. I then look at the way in which judicial procedures have been subject to moralization on the basis of these justifications. And finally, I examine how this affects trials that invoke the death penalty.

In their study on the reasons why Americans have been overwhelmingly supportive of the death penalty for more than fifty years, Phoebe C. Ellsworth and Samuel Gross name the following categories: deterrence, retribution, cost, incapacitation, and emotion (i.e., the argument that some sort of emotional healing results from the death penalty). Only two of these categories are moral (retribution and emotion) and I discuss these in detail below. The other three reasons are pragmatic—and they are all unwarranted. Empirical research has shown that the death penalty in the United States does not have any obvious deterring effect. A survey of deterrence studies by William C. Bailey and Ruth D. Peterson concludes: "Over the decades, the findings from comparative studies were very consistent and quite contrary to the deterrence thesis. . . . Simple comparisons of retentionist and abolitionist jurisdictions showed that the provision for the death penalty had no discernable effect on murder." Even the hardest of hardliners among the intellectual advocates of the death penalty in America, Ernest van den Haag, admits that "statistics have not proved conclusively that the death penalty does or does not deter murder more than other penalties." In line with most other pro–death penalty philosophers, van den Haag soon concedes that deterrence is not the reason why he is in favor of capital punishment, and thus it is ethically irrelevant: "I would be for capital punishment on grounds of justice alone." The popular argument from deterrence is easily dismissed. Not even the theoretical defense of the death penalty is truly concerned with deterrence. Cost is another popular but equally counterfactual pragmatic argument for the death penalty: "Death penalty cases are much more expensive than other criminal cases and cost more than imprisonment for life with no possibility of parole."[6] While economic arguments for the death penalty may well have been (and probably still are) warranted in other countries and societies, they are not in the context of U.S. legal practice. If an American says that he is for the death penalty because it saves taxpayers money, he does not know the facts. The argument for incapacitation is also obviously flawed and, consequently, not taken very seriously by death penalty philosophers. People can be prevented from committing crimes by imprisonment or other measures.

The remaining two arguments, retribution and emotional healing, are essentially *moral*. In fact, the argument from emotion is inseparably connected with the one from retribution—since it is the act of retribution that is supposed to provide emotional comfort for the victims (if they remain among the living), their loved ones, and the rest of society. Still, the argument from retribution can be made on moral grounds (or, in van den Haag's words, "on grounds of justice") alone. The argument from emotion presupposes the argument from retribution, but not vice versa. The retributive impulse has been described as "dominating in public discourse over the past two decades"[7] in the United States and it has been equally dominating in the academic defense of the death penalty.[8] It is typically traced back to Immanuel Kant (and sometimes also to Hegel).[9] Kantian defenders of the death penalty mainly refer to *The Metaphysics of Morals*. (I comment on this interesting treatise in chapter 6.) The very title of this work gives an insight into the Kantian justification of the death penalty. Execution is primarily a moral necessity and only secondarily a matter of law. The death penalty is ultimately seen not as a legal problem, but, expressively, as an ethical one. And, for Kant, the death penalty is necessary because of the moral need for retribution. His pure ethical metaphysics requires it. According to Kant the death penalty is "in accordance with universal laws that are grounded a priori."[10]

The academic defense of the death penalty in the contemporary United States is surprisingly close to Kant, both in method and in content. Just as in Kantian moral metaphysics, the most prominent arguments focus on the moral justification and need for retribution. In one way or another, all death penalty philosophers that I refer to here (van den Haag, Sorell, Burns, and Morris) translate moral principles into legal ones. The death penalty is seen as the legal consequence of the moral need for retribution. Death penalty philosophy in America conceives of itself literally as applied ethics;[11] it assumes that moral principles can and should be the foundation of law and punishment; in other words, it implies that the law needs to consult the philosophers of morality about universal laws that are grounded a priori in order to proceed. This normally is not the case in legal reality—and the legal system does not seem to suffer because of this.

In fact, as far as I can see, legal practice in Europe has largely autonomized itself from moralist fundamentalists. Legal decisions and laws are supposed to be just, but this applied notion of justice in the legal system is highly contingent and cannot be reduced to any metaphysical moral principle or systematic moral philosophy. If I am not mistaken, European jurisprudence does not look at Kantian moral science as the main source of its practice. In other words, legal practice (in many countries) has become too complex, too contingent, and too dynamic to be reduced to a simple set of moral principles. It certainly does not function as the executioner of an indisputable, universal, and a priori ethical need for retribution. The United States is one of the few countries with a notable legal exception, namely the death penalty—at least if one believes the rhetoric of its academic defenders.

The *Metaphysics of Morals* was first published in 1797, not long after the American and French revolutions. At least with respect to law and morality, the United States remains under the spell of the ideas and concepts of the late eighteenth century, and I think this is quite remarkable.

In *The Metaphysics of Morals* Kant argues that punishment by a court acknowledges every human being's innate personality. The innate personality of the criminal requires us to view him not as a mere object but as a fully responsible individual. Thus, wrongdoings can be ascribed to—in Kant's words—the "inner wickedness" (*innere Bösartigkeit*) of the innate personality of the offender. Unlike natural punishment, punishment by a court recognizes the criminal as a person or a free individual. Kant views this recognition as the core of justice, which he fittingly describes in its punitive dimension as the "law of retribution" (*ius talionis, Wiedervergeltungsrecht*). In his typical apodictic manner, Kant insists that *only* the law of retribution can, both quantitatively and qualitatively, determine the punishment of an offender.[12] For Kant *all* legal punishment is derived from the need for retribution, and this, in turn, is founded on a scientific, universal, a priori, and purely reasonable metaphysical account of *ethical* principles. Retributive law is the only morally correct penal law. Only retributive law does justice to the innate personality of the offender and treats him as a free and rational human being. Kantian law and ethical philosophy draw the necessary conclusions from what it means to be truly human. If someone is inherently wicked, then the ethical acknowledgment of his dignity as a free and rational human being necessitates the human right (as well as the legal duty) to execute him.

Kant was not the only "enlightened" person of his time who found it necessary to execute people for the sake of humanity, morality, and reason. His contemporary Maximilien Robespierre was one of the first who not only reflected on these moral issues but also actually came up with a very actively applied ethics.[13] He not only interpreted the world, he set out to change it. I am not implying here that Kant was a Robespierrist—he wasn't. But Robespierre justified his practice of the death penalty in terms that are astoundingly similar to those of Kant. They both shared the belief that justice and the law had to be founded on morality (or virtue in Robespierre's terms) and that morality, in turn, had to be founded on reason. In that sense, the death penalty was, for both Kant and Robespierre, absolutely necessary on the basis of ethical and rational principles, and it reflected human dignity. Kant may not have liked Robespierre's application of this pattern, but their semantic frameworks are remarkably similar. In his last speech to the convention on 26 July 1794, after thousands had been slaughtered during the Reign of Terror, after he had held a grotesque public spectacle to celebrate reason (and shortly before his own execution), Robespierre summed up his moral principles quite concisely: "The French revolution is the first to have been based on the theory of the rights of humanity and the principles of justice. Other revolutions only required ambition; ours imposes virtues." Or in a little more detail:

> Let us not be mistaken: establishing an immense Republic on foundations of reason and equality, holding all the parts of this immense empire together with vigorous bonds, is not an enterprise that can be completed thoughtlessly: it is the masterpiece of virtue and human reason. A host of factions springs up inside a great revolution; how can they be repressed, if you do not subject all the passions to constant justice? Your only guarantor of liberty is rigorous observation of the principles and the universal morality you have proclaimed. If reason does not reign, then crime and ambition must reign.[14]

In this speech, the so-called incorruptible Robespierre defended the executions of his fellow revolutionaries Danton, Fabre, Desmoulins, Hébert, Chaumette, and Ronsin.[15] Their deaths were necessary because they had been conspiring against the rule of humanity, reason, virtue, and the law, and, accordingly, could not be spared—it would be immoral to do this, despite their having been his friends and political allies.

If it had been available to him at the time of the speech, Robespierre might well have referred to a text by Kant on applied ethics in which "the greatest and most punishable crime" is discussed. With respect to this crime, namely rebellion, the death penalty is *absolutely* required: "No rightfully established commonwealth can exist without a force of this kind to suppress all internal resistance. For such resistance would be dictated by a maxim which, if it become general, would destroy the whole civil constitution and put an end to the only state in which men can possess rights. It thus follows that all resistance to the supreme legislative power, all incitement of the subjects to the violent expression of discontent, all defiance which breaks out into rebellion, is the greatest and most punishable crime in the commonwealth, for it destroys its very foundations. This prohibition is absolute." I am not saying that Kant would agree that Robespierre had applied his absolute prohibition in the right way, but I can see how Robespierre could have quoted this passage *word for word* in his self-defense in front of the convention. Robespierre firmly believed that he had acted out of an ethical, moral, and rational necessity. He acted to save "the only state in which men can possess rights" from destruction by the evil foes of these values and virtues. These foes have to suffer capital punishment, and as Robespierre said when he argued in favor of executing Louis XVI, this could well be seen as an act of just and necessary "public vengeance."[16] Many retributionist death penalty defenders do not like to identify retribution with vengeance; some, however, do, for example, Ernest van den Haag and Walter Berns.[17] But when it came to "the greatest and most punishable crime" Robespierre was not shy about using strong words. For both Kant and Robespierre capital punishment was the only reasonable, virtuous, and, on the basis of retribution, appropriate legal response to enemies of the enlightened state.

Contemporary American death penalty philosophers typically suggest some sort of "Kantianism light." They normally do not agree with Kant's insistence on the execution of each and every murderer and rebel and all of their accomplices,[18] but they share his belief that the death penalty is morally necessary. They look at legal justice not as being a contingent social construct, but as the legal application of what can be established as morally just—on the basis of a more or less scientific or rational philosophical analysis. These philosophers are no moral fools. They claim to have identified *the* moral principles of justice, and they expect the legal system to execute these higher principles. Sorell introduces his death penalty philosophy by saying: "Principles that give guidance in decisions about life and death are often moral principles."[19] These ethical experts claim that they are the right people to provide society with guidance in matters of life and death. And this includes the legal system's decisions on capital punishment because they happen to know the principles of morality.

They are also Kantians because of their emphasis on the retributive character of the death penalty. Tom Sorell, explicitly referring to Kant, calls his position "retributivism." Walter Berns, explaining his morality of anger, states that "there is something in the souls of men . . . that requires . . . crimes to be revenged." Van den Haag says: "Particularly in a secular society, we cannot wait for the day of judgment to see murderers consigned to hell. Our courts must 'execute wrath upon him that doeth evil' here and now." Kantian retributivism has become the single most important ethical principle for current death penalty philosophers in the United States. In his interesting book on the history of the death penalty the United States, Stuart Banner says: "Long rejected as a legitimate goal of punishment in academic and policymaking circles, retribution made an astonishingly fast comeback. . . . The point was made again and again—capital punishment was a moral imperative, regardless of whether it reduced the murder rate or cut murderers off from the possibility of rehabilitation."[20]

Finally, the American death penalty philosophers are Kantians because they stress that the death penalty is implied by the moral imperative to respect the human dignity of the offender. If offenders are respected as autonomous human beings equipped with free will and reason, then they have to be granted the fundamental human right of suffering the death penalty. Only the death penalty pays the ultimate respect to the inalienable moral and legal status of the enlightened citizen. Herbert Morris says: "A man has the right to be punished rather than treated [therapeutically] if he is guilty of some offense." And, once more, Ernest van den Haag: "Human beings are human because they can be held responsible, as animals cannot be. In that Kantian sense the death penalty is a symbolic affirmation of the humanity of both victim and murderer."[21]

Contemporary American death penalty philosophers justify capital punishment on the basis of a self-declared moral science of the late eighteenth century that claimed to have scientifically established a priori moral principles, discovered the true nature of human beings, and implied that all social institutions, in particular the law, would have to apply these universal truths if the world was to be enlightened, rational, human, and good. They continue the equally presumptuous and grotesque moral discourse that was fashionable among the moralists of the Enlightenment, and they are as detached from an adequate understanding of contemporary society as those pious men of more than two hundred years ago. Their supposedly timeless, universal, and rational principles do not amount to much more than rhetorical antiquities (or should I say antics?) that deserve to be housed in a museum for intellectual monstrosities.

The infection of legal matters with morality is unfortunately not only a theoretical philosophical problem but also, and this is more worrisome, a practical problem in the courtrooms of the United States. In particular, trials that seek the death penalty are highly charged morally and are thus, in many ways, no longer primarily legal proceedings.

I find it striking how many wrongful convictions have been made especially in cases that involve the death penalty. Here one would expect the utmost scrutiny and care. Statistics show that in the United States wrongful convictions in such cases are not isolated incidents. Notwithstanding the extreme procedural difficulties in having a death penalty verdict reversed, one statistic lists 48 people on death row who, between 1973 and 1993, were released because of innocence.[22] The term "innocent" is here, obviously, used legally, not morally.

The confusion between the moral and legal use of the term "innocence" has become quite prevalent. I discuss this in more detail in chapter 11. Here I emphasize that I find wrongful convictions wrong because of legal and not moral reasons. To convict people for crimes they have not committed is primarily a legal error, and only secondarily, and not even necessarily, a moral error. A convict may not be morally innocent, but she shouldn't be found legally guilty if she is not.

Let me illustrate this with an example from sports. I once took part in a soccer tournament in Germany. Surprisingly, our team reached the finals, and we even scored the winning goal in over-time—or so we thought. The referee annulled the goal for some obscure reason. Shortly after this the other team scored and won the tournament. Afterward, the referee admitted to me that he knew that our goal was allowable and that, technically, we should have won. However, he said this would not have been right since we had played much worse than the other team, not only in the finals but also during the whole tournament. We didn't deserve to win. From a moral perspective he was right. In fact, the other team *was* better and probably *deserved* to win more than we did. But from the perspective of the sports system his decision was obviously wrong. Sports competitions are not decided by morality but by such criteria as the number of goals—scored deservedly or not. In a similar way, wrongful legal convictions may, under special circumstances, actually be morally deserved, but they are still unjust in a legal sense. If he had been a professional referee, everyone would have agreed that he should be fired—he allowed his moral judgment to overrule the criteria constructed within the sports system.

As of the year 2004, 102 people on death row in the United States had been exonerated since 1973.[23] No statistic can tell us how many wrongful convictions remain undetected, how many people remain on death row or have been executed on the basis of a juridical error. One might interpret the high number of exonerations as proof that the system works well—102 innocent people were finally identified. But I think this is a highly dubious claim. It can never be proven, but I believe that this statistic may instead indicate that a similar or even higher number of unlucky inmates were wrongfully executed. In any case, the number certainly indicates that death penalty trials are by no means foolproof. All 102 people had been found guilty beyond a reasonable doubt. How could the juries or the judges in those 102 cases be *without* reasonable doubt? And how could, in each of these cases decided by a jury of twelve people, the verdict be *unanimous*? I think that one of the main reasons for this surprising fact is the moral overkill in U.S. courtrooms, particularly in death penalty cases, and that it is fueled by the recent rise of retributivism.

Typically, the following explanations are offered to explain why a wrongful conviction might have come about: racial prejudice; illegal acts by overzealous prosecutors, police, or judges who misrepresent the facts in order to get a guilty verdict; inadequate counsel because of incompetent court-appointed attorneys or the defendant's inability to pay for an effective defense team. I have no doubt that all these factors have contributed to a good number of wrongful convictions. But I think the strong emphasis on morality that is typically part of U.S. trials involving the death penalty, along with the resurgence of retributivist ethics, probably plays an even more important role.

In "The Symbolic Transformation of American Capital Punishment" Franklin E. Zimring presents an excellent analysis of the shift toward the moralization of death penalty trials in the United States—only he does not call it moralization but "personalization."[24] His term is quite in line with the point I am making. The personal emphasis of current death penalty practice in the United States is a moral emphasis. Whereas in the past the death penalty was justified more by pragmatic, impersonal, and amoral concerns (e.g., deterrence, incapacitation, costs), the focus has now shifted toward a measurement of the "inner wickedness" (to quote Kant again) of the offender and the moral divide that, supposedly, was established through the crime. By committing the crime, the offender has demonstrated his evil character and created an innocent victim. That the victim is called innocent indicates not the obvious truth that she is not legally charged with the crime, but that she did not morally deserve her suffering. Innocence here becomes a moral term. Since the victim is innocent and the offender is wicked, the morality of anger demands retributive justice. The juridical process is transformed into a moral process. It is not so much the legal guilt but the moral guilt that is measured, or supposed to be measured, at the trial. And the distinction between wicked and innocent usually does not leave much room for ambiguities. If someone is found to be evil, it makes good sense to destroy him.

Zimring's analysis of the use of the death penalty in America shows very clearly which recent changes manifest the personalization of death penalty trials, namely, the focus on private interests (or supposed interests) of the victims or their relatives: "The major change in the announced purposes of capital punishment in the United States in the last decades of the twentieth century was the transformation of capital trials and of executions into processes that were thought to serve the personal interests of those closely related to the victims of capital murders. The penalty phase of capital trials has become in many states an occasion for telling the jury its choice of sanction is a measure of the value of the homicide victim's life. . . . The symbolic victim focus at both trial and execution was almost wholly the product of legal innovations and new psychological language that followed the resumption of executions in 1977."[25] When the death penalty was reinstated the semantics of retribution was in fashion. I think this new language of retribution, which has flourished since 1977, is not so much psychological as it is *moral*.

This new focus on the innocence of the victim, on her undeserved suffering, and on the equally undeserved suffering of her relatives became legal reality with the introduction of detailed "victim impact statements" by lawyers and prosecutors, or perhaps even more effectively, directly by relatives and friends of the victim who were called in as character witnesses (or should one say, moral witnesses?). Zimring explains the effect of this shift:

> When the prosecutor elects a capital trial, then the penalty phase is remade into what sociologists call a "status competition" between the offender (whose claims to sympathy and understanding are the subject of his penalty phase presentation) and those who were directly or derivatively injured by the crime. . . . The pro-death-penalty slant in this type of status competition is obvious. Victims and their families are much easier to identify with and offenders are

usually horribly at fault. But the more profound transformation that has occurred is that the penalty phase of the trial is now presented as a competition between the claims of private parties.[26]

And, I would add: as a competition between the moral claims of these parties.

Zimring concludes: "Creating the felt need to commemorate a victim's loss with a death sentence is . . . good for the death penalty. It also obscures the essential governmental nature of both death sentences and executions."[27] Again, I would change the wording slightly: The moral turn of the death penalty trial does not obscure its essential governmental nature, but its essential *legal* nature. The death penalty is, strictly speaking, not a government matter, but a legal matter. And thus the moralization of the trial turns what was supposed to be a legal judgment into a moral judgment.

Zimring then goes on to look at the specific semantics that were created along with the moral/personal shift in capital punishment cases. A new pseudopsychological term was coined: "closure."[28] While the moral shift to victims' interests was obviously a shift toward a morality of retribution, vengeance, or both, these terms do not sound very nice. "Vengeance is an anachronism with a bad press. Something new, something personal, and something that sounded both civilized and refined would be the best candidate for an appealing label for personal involvement in executions. From this perspective, the evocative term 'closure' was a public relations godsend." The term was not used at all in the context of the death penalty before 1989, but since then it has had a fantastic career. It is now quite rare to hear about a death penalty case in the mass media without it being mentioned. As Zimring rightly remarks, the term "has no official function in legislation or legal proceedings"—it is still not a legal concept. But it is of great value for both prosecutors and the mass media in exploiting the moral potential of a murder trial. Zimring cites a poll from 2001 that showed that 60 percent of Americans think that the death penalty is fair because it provides "closure."[29] What a remarkable rating for an argument that didn't exist twelve years earlier!

The term "closure" is used in the American mass media as a good reason to kill evil people—and how could a relative of the victim interviewed on TV not use it? Relatives have learned from the media and prosecutors that they are not only entitled but also expected to yearn for closure if they are to be good victims. Closure has become a symbolic moral necessity. If the media did not speak of closure, the story would lose some of its moral drama. There is no psychological evidence that closure happens through the execution of an offender, but this is, of course, irrelevant since the term is not used psychologically either in the mass media or by the prosecutors. Its function is to express the moral necessity for retribution. Zimring states: "It is not known whether there are psychological advantages in mourning the loss of a loved one when that loss leads to an execution, nor is there any indication that the adjustment to loss of a loved one in a homicide is any different in death penalty states than in non–death penalty states."[30] Some states even go so far as to let a victim's relatives witness the execution of an offender for the sake of closure. I can hardly imagine how this could be psychologically beneficial. Closure is a psychological phantom, but an extremely efficient moral and rhetorical device in U.S. death penalty practice and media coverage.

A last important observation about "the transformation of execution into a victim service gesture" made by Zimring is that "it links the symbolism of execution to a long American history of community control of punishment."[31] Zimring documents in great detail how the current U.S. practice of the death penalty is related to earlier forms of community control of punishment, namely lynching and vigilantism. The moral cult of the innocent victim and the evil offender historically connects current legal practice not with the legal system but with extralegal (and now illegal) acts of public violence that were once seen as morally right. The moralization of trials that involve the death penalty makes them less a purely legal procedure than a new form of public—constituted by the mass media—lynching.

What I have said so far about such moralization may explain why the death penalty is still so popular in the United States, but it does not yet sufficiently support my initial hypothesis that it also plays a major role with respect to wrongful convictions. After all, the moral sympathy for capital punishment does not translate into a moral sympathy for wrongful capital punishment. Obviously, I do not mean to say that the judges or juries who impose wrongful convictions are somehow morally inclined to have an innocent person killed. What I am saying is it is easier to find someone legally guilty when they are seen or presented as morally guilty. While in most wrongful convictions cases there must have been some room for legal doubt (after all, in each instance the wrong person was convicted), there was likely little room for moral doubt. To cite Walter Berns again: "There is something in the souls of men . . . that requires . . . crimes to be revenged."[32] I do not know if there is something like this in the souls of men, but there is certainly something in communication in the courtroom and the mass media that makes judges and jurors decide that revenge is a moral necessity—that the evil one must be killed.

Typically, a death penalty trial in the United States consists of two phases: the "guilt phase" and the "sentencing phase." The first phase is only meant to determine if the defendant is actually guilty of the crime. At this stage the question of whether the death penalty should actually be imposed is not yet to be considered. In the second phase, the guilt of the defendant is not to be questioned; it is now regarded as proven beyond a reasonable doubt. Here the only issue for the jury (which is usually the same as in the first phase) is if the death penalty should be imposed. Joseph L. Hoffman explains the substantial difference in the jury's tasks in the two stages and outlines how a legal process turns into a moral one: "At the sentencing phase of a trial . . . the jury is no longer deciding a question that has a 'true' or 'false' answer. Instead the jury is being asked to decide a moral question that has no 'true' or 'false' answer: Is the defendant a person who deserves to live or to die. This is not a question of fact but one of moral judgment. There are no rules for making this kind of decision, and the law gives the jury no definitive guidance."[33] In the sentencing phase, legal issues hardly matter any longer. The only question that remains is, Is it morally right to kill the defendant?

One does not have to wonder what the sentencing phase looks like—you can see it on TV in a true crime show: The prosecution tries to create moral outrage in the jury by comparing the wicked offender with the innocent victim. It focuses on victim impact statements to show that the moral chasm opened up by the crime can only be closed by a verdict of death. The defense pleads for mercy and asks the jury to consider that the offender is not really responsible for having become so evil, that there were circumstances beyond his control. Or the defense may say that while the deed was evil, the offender is not—or, in the meantime, has repented. Two purely moral claims face one another. The jury becomes the audience of a moral spectacle and then has to decide—*without definitive guidance by the law*—between a morality of retribution and a morality of mercy. At this stage the law leaves the decision about life and death entirely to the moral inclinations of a group of more or less arbitrarily selected people. In short: When it comes to the final word on the death penalty, the law retreats almost entirely and allows a moral contest: "The trial judge's power to override the jury's sentencing verdict is (in most states) extremely limited."[34]

Here is how a prosecutor speaks to the jury during the sentencing phase to obtain a death verdict. The case concerns the murder of a young mother named Charisse and her daughter Lacie Jo. It was witnessed by her son Nicholas who survived the assault:

> There is nothing you can do to ease the pain of any of the families involved in this case. There is nothing you can do to ease the pain of Bernice or Carl Payne [parents of the defendant], and that's a tragedy. There is nothing you can do basically to ease the pain of Mr. and Mrs. Zvolanek [adult victim's parents], and that's a tragedy. They will have to live with it the rest of their lives. There is obviously nothing you can do for Charisse and Lacie Jo. But there is something that you can do for Nicholas.
>
> Somewhere down the road Nicholas is going to grow up, hopefully. He's going to want to know what happened. And he is going to know what happened to his baby sister and his mother. He is going to want to know what happened. With your verdict, you will provide the answer.[35]

Franklin E. Zimring analyzes what happened in this case: "The prosecutor . . . presents himself as *Nicholas's* lawyer instead of the *state's* lawyer. The jury is being asked to make its only choice in the penalty trial by vindicating and recognizing the loss of a little boy. The implication of this type of argument is that the selection of a sentence other than death in this phase of the trial would be a direct rejection of the interests of Nicholas Christopher."[36] The jury is addressed as some sort of God-like entity that must enact moral justice through personal vengeance. The jurors are addressed as if it were their indisputable moral duty to come up with a death verdict, and if they do not, they themselves would be immoral! The only way for the jurors to preserve their own morality is to call for the execution of the offender. If the jury does not do this, it continues the suffering of the victim and becomes a partner in this crime. How many jurors are able to withstand this enormous moral pressure?

Nearly one-third of all jurors in such cases who were surveyed in an empirical study believed that the law required them to impose the death penalty, whereas in fact "under the law of almost all states, a jury is *never* required to impose a death sentence on a defendant; the trial judge instructs the jury that the proper sentence in a capital case is *always* a matter of jury discretion."[37] Obviously, these jurors have misinterpreted, likely under the influence of the prosecution, a legal possibility as a moral requirement. They were fooled into thinking that their moral judgment was legally prescribed. It was not, but moral discourse had already brainwashed them.

Given the moral quest for retribution that underlies the sentencing phase, it is no wonder that a jury will easily disregard evidence or other legal matters that are in favor of a defendant—after all, this is no longer an issue since guilt has already been established and is not to be reviewed. What counts here is ethics, and ethics alone. Under these circumstances, there is no legal recourse for the wrongfully convicted. At this stage, exoneration is impossible and so an innocent and a guilty person are equally likely to receive the death penalty.

Still, one could argue that since the guilt phase is separated from the sentencing phase, the latter cannot really be blamed for the mistakes of the former. It seems that wrongful convictions originate in the guilt phase—when the guilt is wrongly established—and that this is not a result of moral discourse in the sentencing phase but of legal error in the guilt phase. However, it is an illusion that moral arguments do not play a major role in the guilt phase as well. While there is obviously more emphasis on evidence and other legal matters in the guilt phase than in the sentencing phase, this does not mean in practice that there is less moral discourse. The only difference between the two phases in this respect is that while the sentencing phase is entirely moral, the guilt phase is only partly moral. According to the empirical study mentioned above, nearly 65 percent of the jurors who were interviewed "reported discussing their feelings about the right punishment during the . . . guilt phase deliberations."[38] Technically, a jury is supposed to reflect during the guilt phase of a trial only on the issue of the defendant's guilt that has to be proven beyond a reasonable doubt. Despite this, the jury is exposed to a wide variety of arguments from the prosecution concerning victim impact statements, the personal character of the offender, moral outrage about the nature of the crime, and so on that have little to do with the actual guilt of the offender. In violation of the legal idea of the guilt phase, the prosecution tries to direct the jury's attention away from this amoral question to the question of what punishment is morally deserved. And this obviously works quite well. The prosecution typically stresses the moral aspects of the case even during the guilt phase in order to obtain a guilty verdict.

Moral polarization is not less effective in obtaining a guilty verdict than in obtaining a death sentence: "Emotional arguments by lawyers, pressures from the mass media, and personal disagreements within the jury room often seem to distort jury decision making."[39] The emotional arguments mentioned here are in fact mainly moral arguments. The jury's emotions are stirred and manipulated by the prosecution and the press. Moral outrage is as good a rhetorical weapon in the guilt phase as in the sentencing phase. Just as a jury in the sentencing phase may impose a death penalty on a defendant on moral grounds, it may impose a guilty verdict in the guilt phase for the same reason. It is an illusion that the guilt phase is morally clean and only focuses on fact-finding.

Since the death penalty in the United States is seen as morally necessary in the context of retribution and closure, every capital punishment case there is morally tainted from the beginning. Once the prosecution decides to seek the death penalty it has already, for all practical purposes, introduced a moral framework into the case. Since the death penalty is not so much about criminals as it is about evildoers, no phase of the trial can be concerned only with the amoral facts—moral facts play a decisive role throughout the whole trial. In my view this is probably a major reason for the extent of wrongful convictions in capital punishment cases. These cases, more than any other type, are inherently infected by morality that may well make reasonable doubt a moral matter rather than a matter of hard evidence.

The now anachronistic U.S. jury system invites excessive moral discourse and a limitation of legal discourse. The jury members are not legal experts, so the prosecution and defense fight for the jury's moral approval. This is, in varying degrees, true for every trial decided by jury. Cases that involve the death penalty are highly moral from the beginning, and so tend to be among the most moral and least legal of trials. Therefore, arguably, they are more prone to legal errors than others.

The following passage is from a speech by the prosecution to the jury in the case of Kerry Max Cook. It led to his wrongful conviction—a conviction based on shaky evidence, and put him on death row for twenty-two years. . Finally, a DNA analysis proved his innocence. The quote is taken from the play *The Exonerated*. According to the authors "with a few exceptions, each spoken word in this play comes from the public record—legal documents, court transcripts, letters—or from an interview with an exonerated person."[40] I thus assume that the following passage is authentic:

Ladies and Gentlemen of the Jury. I would be remiss in my duty if I did not show you every last grotesque detail because the killer sits right before you in this courtroom and it is time for twelve good people from this country to put that man on the scrap heap of humanity where he belongs. He has a warped perversion and he will not reason with you. The victim was a young woman just beginning to realize her dreams and he butchered her body. This is the kind of sick perversion that turns Kerry Max Cook on. You people have no right to even submit prison guards to the kind of risk that man poses. Think about it. Do you want to give this pervert his butcher knife back? Now, we must look upon it as putting a sick animal to sleep. Kerry Max Cook has forfeited his right to walk among us. He no longer has rights. So let's let all the freaks and perverts and murderous homosexuals of the world know what we do with them in a court of justice. That we take their lives.[41]

In this case, "twelve good people from this country" did their moral duty and put Mr. Cook "on the scrap heap of humanity." They did what the prosecution asked them to do, namely let "all the freaks and perverts and murderous homosexuals of the world know what we do with them in a court of justice. That we take their lives." This is indeed what, in the United States, is done in a court of justice. The question I pose here is, Are these truly courts of legal justice or are they instead courts of a morally infected justice?

The main hypothesis of this chapter is that morality is not a solution to but part of the problem of capital punishment in the United States. A possible counterargument would be: But aren't there also moral mechanisms within the U.S. penal process that are against the death penalty? There is the right of state governors to grant clemency to convicted offenders or even a moratorium on executions altogether. Isn't this a way in which morality corrects itself? But the opposite seems to be the case. Currently, moral reasoning is overwhelmingly used to justify not clemency, but the refusal to grant clemency or declare a moratorium. The current function of moral discourse with respect to clemency is not to exert it, but to prevent it. In other words: Clemency is, in contemporary American death penalty rhetoric, typically depicted as less moral than retribution. There has been a "nothing if not spectacular" decline in executive clemency since 1977.[42] I presume that the reason for this is the triumph of retributivist morality.

Executive clemency has to be granted by politicians. It is, strictly speaking, not a legal, but a political act. Since politicians desire to be elected or reelected, they tend to present themselves in line with the dominant moral discourse in their constituency. If they do not do this, they run a political risk. The death penalty has been consistently favored by a large majority of Americans during the past fifty years, and its current popularity is immediately connected with a retributivist morality. Retribution and closure are seen as the most important moral bases for the death penalty. A politician who grants executive clemency will thus be seen as either immoral or at least as

not moral enough, particularly in the mass media where the death penalty enjoys a high moral prestige. Stuart Banner writes in his history of capital punishment in America: "For an elected official to disagree with that sentiment in public was often tantamount to giving up hope of continuing one's career. The most visible example took place during the 1988 presidential election, when Michael Dukakis was widely believed to have lost any chance of winning after he emphasized his opposition to capital punishment during a debate against George Bush. Four years later, in the midst of the 1992 campaign, Bill Clinton made it a point to return to Arkansas to sign the death warrant for Ricky Rector, a brain-damaged inmate so oblivious to his fate that he planned to save the dessert from his last meal to eat after his execution."[43]

With respect to moratoriums, Franklin E. Zimring reports the following case: "In Nebraska, the state legislature enacted a memorandum on executions in 1999 pending study of the fairness and reliability of that state's death penalty system. In vetoing the moratorium law, Governor Michael Johanns tells us: 'I feel strongly that part of my role as Governor is to do all I can to carry out the law for the benefit of the victims and their families. . . . The moratorium would be just one more roadblock to bringing closure for them.' "[44]

Machiavelli remarked that "a prince must want to have a reputation for compassion rather than for cruelty."[45] But what public opinion considers compassionate or cruel is highly contingent. There were times when a political figure would appear compassionate if he granted clemency to a person about to be executed. This seems to have been the case in the United States when executive clemency was relatively frequent (i.e., before 1976). Today, a politician is seen as compassionate if he does *not* grant clemency, compassionate not to the offender, of course, but to the victims. In accordance with the morality of retribution, ethical compassion is demonstrated by not being "cruel" to victims by halting an execution. There is nothing in morality or compassion that would necessarily lead to an anti–death penalty view.

Larry Myers presents an interesting account of the futile legal efforts to have the death penalty verdict for Herbert Lamont Otey commuted into a sentence of life without parole. The details of the case are quite fascinating but I focus here only on its political and moral aspects. The whole case was highly politicized and attracted considerable media attention. Attorney General Stenberg, a staunch supporter of the death penalty, "occasionally used the victim's family members standing behind him as a backdrop for his television press conferences." The clemency process had turned into a political and moral mass media show, and this show had little to do with the law. According to Myers, Otey said to a friend a week before his execution: "If I die, it will be a political killing."[46] Of course, he was right. But it was a political killing for *moral* reasons. In this case, both the law and politics were overpowered by moral communication.

The current U.S. position on clemency morality leads us back to the one who started it all, the moral metaphysician Immanuel Kant. With him we find the blueprint for the contemporary attitude toward executive clemency. The right to grant executive clemency, according to Kant, has no place in a truly moral law. For Kant it is highly unjust.[47] If one reflects on the cases outlined above, it seems that U.S. governors share his perspective. Maybe they should abolish the clemency process altogether since it is, given the Kantian retributive moral imperative, immoral to begin with.

11 | MASTERS OF WAR

THE *DAODEJING* (OR *LAOZI*) is among the oldest and most influential texts that presents a philosophy of war, or more precisely, the art of war. There was a whole school of war philosophy in ancient China and translations of their treatises are quite popular in the West today.[1] East Asian martial arts—which also now enjoy great popularity in the West—are rooted in this tradition. One of the many remarkable differences between Daoist reflections on war and those that appear in the Western tradition is the profoundly *amoral* way in which war is approached in texts like the *Daodejing*,[2] as opposed to the often highly ethical war philosophies in the Occidental tradition.[3] Daoist philosophy is nonanthropocentric and certainly does not look at humans as the measure of all things. It views social issues, including war, in the context of heaven and earth, that is in the context of nature—or the cosmos—as a whole. And nature is, from this point of view, morally foolish; it does not function in an ethical way. War is accordingly not presented in humanist terms as a moral issue, as a fight between good and evil forces, between just and unjust interests, between heroes and villains. Many chapters in the *Daodejing* either explicitly or implicitly mention warfare, but none deals with it moralistically in terms of right and wrong.

In Daoism, war appears as an unhealthy and unfruitful conflict of forces, as a terrible waste of social energies, as the most severe and devastating form of disorder in society, as a social catastrophe. It can be likened to natural catastrophes or fatal diseases. It indicates a total breakdown or interruption of productive processes. Rain, in nature, makes things grow. A hailstorm, however, can devastate the harvest. Just as a hailstorm indicates a breakdown of natural order and interrupts the usual cycle of natural and agricultural reproduction and growth, war interrupts all productive and reproductive social processes. It is merely destructive. The function of Daoist statecraft is to guarantee order in the social realm. War is therefore seen as the greatest possible failure of rulership. It is the worst possible outcome of failed politics. War is, indeed, terribly bad—but, interestingly, not evil. To say that war is evil would, from a Daoist perspective, be as strange as saying that an earthquake is evil. An earthquake cannot be judged morally—and, at least for the Daoists, the same is true for war.

The Daoists were quite realistic with respect to warfare. While they saw the main function of political rule as preserving social order and productivity—and thus *preventing* war—they accepted the fact that war happens. War happens just as hailstorms, earthquakes, and bodily illness happen. If it cannot be prevented—and for the Daoists prevention is always much more important and efficient than treatment after the fact—then it has to be dealt with and its harm has to be minimized. The Daoists abhorred war, but they were no pacifists. Although they saw war as a terrible political failure, they also saw that it could not, like earthquakes or sicknesses simply be eradicated. In case of war, a Daoist ruler would try to win with the least possible damage. Daoist war strategy relies on defense and evasion. A successful campaign would have the enemy overextend himself. With his energies exhausted, his armies would collapse. Daoist war strategy does not aim at overpowering the enemy, but at making the enemy overpower himself. Again, one can compare the state of war with physical illness. One does not literally fight a fever. It is more effective to evade it by resting.

What I emphasize again is that, from such a perspective, it makes no sense to look at war ethically. War is always a bad thing—but it is not evil. If war could be called evil, it could also be labeled good or just. For the Daoists war is not evil, but it is always, in an amoral sense, wrong. It is as wrong as a hailstorm or a fever, and it makes no sense to qualify it ethically. Normally, no one (with the exception of some religious fanatics) will call a hailstorm or a fever just. Consequently, there is no reason at all for thinking that a war is just or right.

In stark contrast to Daoism, the Western philosophical tradition has strongly emphasized the moral aspects of warfare.[4] Just war theory dates back at least to Augustine's *City of God*, but it can also be traced to ancient Greece or Rome. There are, to be sure, also strategic approaches to warfare in the Western tradition (one may think of Machiavelli and von Clausewitz), but these remained at the fringes of what was considered philosophy. Philosophically, ethical (and religious) issues were normally seen as more important than merely practical deliberations about how to win a war. This difference once more shows that, generally speaking, Chinese philosophy, and specifically Daoism, was more concerned with efficacy than with truth. Daoist philosophy focused much more on how to deal with war than on defining the characteristics of a truly good or just war.

Here I limit my discussion and criticism of Western just war theory to its most prominent contemporary representative, Michael Walzer. I cannot say to what extent Walzer's theory is representative of the rich tradition of Western war ethics, but as I see it, he follows in the footsteps of modern ethical philosophers like Kant and Bentham (see chapter 6), who try to identify their principles of goodness or justice. Walzer's principles are certainly less transcendental than Kant's and less mathematical than Bentham's, but he is still optimistic enough to assume that he can come up with a number of "practical" (in his words) insights into the basic morality of warfare.

Walzer explicitly points out that his approach to warfare is not legal but ethical. He does not focus on the legal justness of a war. In the preface to *Just and Unjust Wars* he says: "This is not a book about the positive laws of war." Instead, Walzer is "concerned precisely with the present structure of the moral world." He intends "to recapture the just war for political and moral theory" and, with respect to war, wants to analyze "moral claims, seek out their coherence, lay bare the principles that they exemplify."[5]

As many just war theorists have done and continue to do, Walzer distinguishes between *jus ad bellum* (the right to make war) and *jus in bello* (the rights of engagement in war)—but he uses the term "right" (*jus*) in its moral and not in its legal meaning. I am not very concerned with the distinction between *jus ad bellum* and *jus in bello*, since I think that conceiving of them in a moral—as opposed to a legal—sense is precisely where the problem lies. I again argue for the separation of law and morality. I do not think that Walzer's moral approach to both rights is very helpful.

Walzer admits how difficult it is to adequately judge which wars and which acts of war can be labeled "just." Since there are so many different circumstances under which wars are fought, it is not easy to find general moral principles that do justice to all the individual cases. He devotes a great deal of attention to specific historical incidents and attempts to come up with rather complex evaluations of the moral character of each war he examines. I mention only a few of these evaluations that broadly represent Walzer's position.

According to Walzer, the Second World War was just for the allies and unjust for the Axis. Within the Axis, the war of the Nazis was more unjust than that of the Japanese, because the former were "an ultimate threat to everything decent in our lives" and "immeasurably awful." It was therefore a moral duty to wage war against the Nazis, and in this special case—although Walzer normally condemns the killing of noncombatants—bombing raids against German cities were just. These raids were just only as long as they fulfilled a military purpose (although some people argue that this was never the case) and in the case of an "extreme emergency" because a "determinate crime (the killing of innocent people)" has to be measured "against that immeasurable evil (a Nazi triumph)." With reference to Japan, American use of atomic weapons was unjust because the Japanese "had never posed such a threat to peace and freedom as the Nazis had."[6]

The U.S. war in Vietnam was unjust because it was in support of an illegitimate government that otherwise would not have been able to sustain itself. Here Walzer states: "A legitimate government is one that can fight its own internal wars. And external assistance in those wars is rightly called counter-intervention only when it balances, and does no more than balance, the prior intervention of another power, making it possible once again for the local forces to win or lose on their own."[7]

Other foreign interventions, however, have been just. The Indian invasion of Bangladesh in 1971 was just because the Pakistani forces committed massacres and "people who initiate massacres lose their right to participate in the normal (even in the normally violent) process of domestic self-determination. Their military defeat is morally necessary."[8]

The Israeli attack on Egypt that started the Six-Day War in 1967 was just, even though it was an act of aggression—which, according to Walzer, is normally unjust. In this case it was just because Egypt planned to destroy Israel and thus the Israeli first strike was "a clear case of legitimate anticipation." The moral principle that justifies the Israeli attack is, "States may use military force in the face of threats of war, whenever the failure to do so would seriously risk their territorial integrity or political independence."[9]

The most obvious counterargument against Walzer's position is relativistic in nature. Walzer discusses this argument in detail with reference to Hobbes and the *Leviathan*, whom he quotes as saying that categories such as fairness and justice are "ever used with relation to the person that useth them"; and that "one calleth wisdom, what another calleth fear; and one cruelty what another justice. . . . And therefore such names can never be true grounds of any ratiocination."[10] Indeed, one may question many of Walzer's moral judgments from such a Hobbesian-relativist perspective. Would the Chinese, for instance, agree with Walzer that the Japanese weren't as bad as the Nazis and therefore had to be dealt with on the basis of different moral principles? Couldn't the Chinese claim that to them, the Japanese were an immeasurable evil? What would an Arab just war theoretician say about Israel's attack on Egypt? Couldn't Arab just war theoreticians use Walzer's definition of the legitimacy of governments to point out the illegitimacy of the Israeli government because its military supremacy is based on outside support that prevents the local forces from winning or losing on their own? I certainly am not suggesting that such possible rationales are better than Walzer's, but Hobbes seems to be right. It is rather difficult to reach moral agreement on these matters.

Walzer is opposed to relativism and basically agrees with the following assumptions that Jean Bethke Elshtain ascribes to contemporary "just war thinkers as layers-down-of the law," namely, the "existence of universal moral dispositions," "the need for moral judgments of who/what is aggressor/victim, just/unjust," and "the potential efficacy of moral appeals and arguments."[11] Walzer's moral arguments read like final and universal moral propositions and make clear distinctions between who is ultimately just and who is not. From a relativist and, I would say empirical, perspective, Walzer's epistemological optimism about his own ability to identify certain moral principles that are universally valid is unwarranted. These principles cannot be and are not unequivocally applicable. They are always open to conflicting interpretations. Robert L. Holmes illustrates this problem with a shocking example:

> *Mein Kampf* represents the German nation (meaning the German people, not the state) as confronting the very kind of threat to its survival and values that Walzer takes to justify supreme emergencies and that just war theorists almost universally take to constitute a just cause. Hitler saw the German nation as threatened by a Marxist-Jewish conspiracy of diabolical proportions, sapping its life, poisoning its blood, and dragging it down from its prior heights of cultural achievement. . . . That he was mistaken in these views is beside the point. One acts necessarily upon what he *believes*. People can only apply principles that seem to them relevant. And this allows for error. So, if one lays down such requirements for a just war as that one have a just cause, what this means in practice is that nations may resort to war when they *believe* they have a just cause.[12]

I think that Holmes' criticism is an even more powerful reply to Walzer than Hobbesian relativism. I think that Holmes is perfectly right in pointing out that Hitler believed in the ultimate moral rightness of his wars and his genocide because he thought there was a Marxist-Jewish conspiracy that would lead to the total destruction of Germany if he did not oppose it violently—and he managed to make most Germans and many outside Germany share this belief for a time. One can certainly say the belief was wrong, but as Holmes points out, this is irrelevant because one has access only to beliefs, not to truths, and one will always believe that which one believes is true.

The crucial issue is therefore not merely that just war arguments are open to interpretation and that what seems just to one person or community may seem highly unjust to others. The issue is also that just war theory is factually applied by well-meaning thinkers such as Walzer and, probably with the same intense belief in its validity, by such people as Adolf Hitler. Hitler was, one could argue, quite successful at promoting his just war theory: He induced millions to act on it. In other words, the problem is not only that the universal validity of moral judgments is highly questionable, but also, and probably more importantly, that the belief in such a validity invariably and irrespective of its objective validity factually divides the world into those who deserve to live and those who deserve to die.

Just war theory is not merely an academic issue for professional moralists; it is typically applied as a rhetorical device, as a rhetorical *weapon*, in war. It represents one of the most dangerous uses of morality as a communications tool.[13] In wartime, just war theory, popularized by the mass media, politicians, the army, churches, moral philosophers, and public opinion is the counterpart of the weapons industry. It is, more or less inescapably, part of the war machine. There is hardly a time when morality is more virulent in a society than during wartime. War typically goes along not only with material explosions but also with explosions of morality, detonations of moral discourse. Just war theory is the most explosive ethics of all.

Walzer devotes many pages to morally condemning terrorism, particularly in his book *Arguing about War,* which was published in 2004 and was written, in part, after 9/11.[14] Walzer gives a concise definition of what terrorism is for him: It "is the deliberate killing of innocent people, at random, in order to spread fear through a whole population and force the hand of its political leaders." He admits that this definition best fits national liberation or revolutionary movements (such as the IRA, FLN, PLO, ETA), but he also holds that it should include state terrorism either against one's own population (as with military dictatorships in South America) or against foreign civilians (Hiroshima). He explicitly disagrees with the idea that "one man's terrorist is another man's freedom fighter" and cites the case of the Battle of Algiers when Algerian terrorists targeted French civilians: "In the 1960s, when someone from the FLN put a bomb in a café where French teenagers gathered to flirt and dance and called himself a freedom fighter, only fools were fooled."[15] Well, I am a moral fool, and was fooled myself while watching *The Battle of Algiers*, a film by Gillo Pontecorvo that documents the Algerian terrorist war of independence so well.

My problem with Walzer's view of terrorism is that it is based on the moral notion of innocence that is still so popular within theoretical and applied just war ethics. "Innocence" is an arbitrary ascription. It is a contingent attribute that is constructed by moral discourse. Legally, civilians are obviously innocent, but so are soldiers, including the one who dropped the bomb on Hiroshima. Still, just war theorists like Walzer do not use this term in a legal, but in a moral way. However, were the French teenagers who "gathered to flirt and dance" really innocent victims from the perspective of the FLN? Obviously not. To begin with, the French had first targeted innocent Algerians, so that, from the point of view of retributive justice (see chapter 10) the act could well be morally defended. (I am not defending it from this perspective since I do not believe in retributive justice—but neither does Walzer.) More importantly, though, the Algerians did point out that they would have preferred a conventional war but were denied this option because the French occupier's military was so superior. The French occupation forces, to use Walzer's own terminology, made it impossible "for the local forces to win or lose on their own." The sympathizers of a French Algeria, mostly constituted by the French expatriates, were backed by a foreign police and military machine that could not be confronted directly by the FLN. This resulted in the extreme type of asymmetric warfare that is usually the military precondition for what Walzer defines as terrorism. The unjust tactics of terrorism were simply a reaction to the equally unjust (according to Walzer's own criteria) circumstances of the foreign military occupation.

From the perspective of the FLN and its native supporters the innocence of the French teenagers (there were, in fact, not only teenagers in the cafe, of course) was highly questionable. After all, they were among the actual foreign invaders. They were the very reason for the presence of the foreign police and military apparatus directed against native Algerians. They were not neutral or passive in any meaningful sense of the word; they *were* the occupying population. I do not see why the Algerians would have conceived of them as innocent if they choose to apply a moral framework to the conflict. From their perspective, it made some sense to look at the French living in Algiers as the very agents of suppression.

Walzer creates the popular illusion of just war theory: there are clear black-and-white differences between those who are morally innocent and those who are guilty, between the victims and the aggressors. But were the victims of the bombings in Germany and Hiroshima really innocent? On the one hand, I suppose that most of them were not only active political supporters of the Nazis or the Japanese government but also, in one way or another, practically involved in the aggressive warfare of their countries—which is unavoidable in times of total mobilization. On the other hand, were they really guilty? Did they not try simply to save their country, their families, their own lives? They did not start the war themselves. Perhaps they had become victims of an evil political force. I am too much of a moral fool to see clear innocence or guilt in the French in Algiers in the 1960s or the Germans living in the cities that were bombed in World War II. I am not sure if it makes sense to determine their fate on the basis of moral terms and come to a definite conclusion on whether their deaths were justified.

According to Walzer, the Iraq war of Bush the elder was, all in all, morally justified—except the taking of innocent life.[16] In Walzer's view, the civilians killed by Americans in Iraq were innocent—but what about the tens or perhaps hundreds of thousands of Iraqi soldiers who were killed by American firepower? Why were they so much more guilty than those who happened not to be enlisted in the army? And what about the moral status of the U.S. soldiers who had voluntarily joined the army and served in a war that resembled a turkey shoot? With very little risk for their own safety American soldiers could kill thousands of more or less helpless Iraqi soldiers sent out by a ruthless dictator. According to the *World Almanac and Book of Facts, 1998*, there were 299 deaths (148 battle deaths, and 151 other deaths) among the 467,939 American soldiers involved in the war. The likelihood of dying for a U.S. soldier was 0.06 percent. It was *safer* for an American to be a soldier in Iraq than to spend a year as a civilian in her own capital. Washington, D.C.'s, murder rate per 100,000 people was 73.1 in 1998, that is, 0.073 percent, and this number refers only to battle deaths, so to speak, not to other deaths (from traffic accidents, for instance)![17]

Was this just warfare simply because, technically speaking, the conflict was between two regular armies? Were these two armies, morally and militarily, in any sense comparable? Walzer never speaks of the ridiculously uneven death toll, a death toll even more lop-sided than in Vietnam where fewer than 60,000 U.S. deaths were met by between 1 million and 3 million Vietnamese, Cambodian, and Laotian deaths (i.e., between 20 and 60 dead locals for each American). In Iraq, though the U.S. military seems to have been careful not to count the enemy's losses so that it is very difficult to obtain reliable numbers, it seems realistic to assume that there were about 100 Iraqis killed for every U.S. soldier.[18] Don't these numbers come close to what can be called a massacre? But perhaps, in line with Walzer's argumentation, we can call this a just massacre. It should not be too difficult for him to come up with a just massacre theory as well.

What I am saying is that the moral category of innocence that is very much at the heart of Walzer's thought and specifically of his antiterrorism ethics, is nothing but a communicative construct—it is not measurable or identifiable and, as it is applied, functions as a *weapon*. The distinction between the guilty and the innocent is, in Walzer's theory, the distinction between those who can be killed and those who can't. Its function is to complement and to direct the real weapons. Just as guns and axes are dangerous tools, so too is just war theory. Just war theory is the communicative means that func-tions to aim the guns and axes. The problem here is not—as stated in the introduction—one of abuse. The terminology of abuse is sim-ply a variation of the terminology of innocence. If a gun is aimed at the innocent it is said to be abused. But in fact, both guns and just war theory function equally well if used or abused. There is nothing in the things themselves that determines their use or abuse. It is sim-ply a matter of how we speak about them. The question is, Is this kind of communication really helpful? Gun control is a means of restricting the use of guns and thus minimizing both their use and abuse. It is largely abolished during wartime. I would call for just war theory control to restrict the use of communicative embellish-ment of weapon usage—but such control would probably be im-possible in wartime. Perhaps one could, at least, call for treaties to block the proliferation of just war theories in addition to those treaties that already prevent the proliferation of weapons of mass destruction.

The criteria introduced by Walzer to evaluate the moral justness of a war are highly problematic and simplistic. Innocence and guilt are not as easily discernible as he assumes. The same holds true for the distinction between noncombatants and combatants in conflicts such as those in Algeria or Israel-Palestine. Similarly, the concepts of terrorism, aggression, defense, and preemptive strike are not always as clear-cut as they seem, and they are certainly difficult to morally accept or condemn on principle. Walzer's reduction of war to a moral issue is not at all useful for understanding the social complexities that are involved. War is not *primarily* a moral issue—as he implies. Wars do not happen in a merely moral world, but in a world where economic, political, religious, ethnic, territorial, and cultural interests clash. And none of these interests are primarily moral. To have or not to have oil, to support democracy or communism, to be Shia or Sunni, Serbian or Croatian, to be the occupier or the occupied, to be for or against a certain lifestyle—all these issues can matter in war, but none of them can be adequately reduced to a clear moral dualism between good and evil. Walzer assumes that his principles can provide a formula for translating nonmoral distinctions into moral distinctions. I do not think that he is very successful. He either simply ignores many factors that play an important role in conflict or reduces them to a moral dimension. In this way he comes up with a very poor and one-sided analysis of warfare.

Walzer's translation of the complexities of war into an ethical narrative makes war into a fairy tale. It is like the clash between worthy knights and shrewd villains. This is not very useful for a theoretical, analytical, or philosophical understanding of war, but it is very useful for arguing about war in public, or, more precisely, in politics and the mass media. This fairy-tale version makes people listen to speeches and watch films and TV. It is an important tool for making conflict popular and for artificially dividing the world into us and them.

I think that terrorism and just war theory have a lot in common. One important function of terrorism, as can be seen in the case of the Battle of Algiers, is that it clarifies and intensifies the distinction between the innocent and the guilty, a distinction that, interestingly enough, people are relatively unconcerned with in normal life. In peacetime we do not tend to conceive of others in terms of moral innocence or guilt. I, for one, do usually not classify people I deal with in a general sense as guilty or innocent and thus as deserving to be killed/not deserving to be killed. Terrorism, I believe, has the function of establishing this abnormal distinction in society. Terrorists try to demonstrate that some people actually deserve to be killed. Their actions are often intended to provoke harsh counter-reactions, so that even more people will believe in the guilt of their opponent.

Probably most Algerians did not particularly like the French occupation and the French occupiers, but still, before terrorism, they would not have conceived of them as guilty in the sense of deserving to be killed. Once the FLN had provoked strong military action on behalf of the French, more and more people changed their minds about this. Terrorism has the effect of propagating the guilty/innocent distinction in society. It transforms others into deserving military targets and shows where the guns should be aimed. The function of just war theory is very similar, or at least complementary, to terrorism. It invites us to look at the world in terms that we normally hesitate to apply. In a war this seems to be necessary if one believes that it cannot be fought very effectively on the basis of everyday amorality. Armies tend to disallow moral foolishness. Terrorism and just war theory help make us morally smart.

The ancient Daoists did not care much for moral smartness and war. They were interested in avoiding and preventing war, and thus aimed at preserving moral foolishness as long as possible. For them, moral smartness was not a good thing; it was already a symptom of social crisis and an indicator of potential conflict.

In this context one may also think of other non-Western and nonethical practices of warfare. Warfare was an important part of the social life of Native Americans. Raids on other groups, which often involved stealing horses, were frequent in many tribes and considered as proof of manhood, strength, and daring. Violence and cruelty were also an important part of the social life of many communities. I do not know that these violent and sometimes cruel acts were considered to be just in any sense comparable to just war theory. It does not seem to me that just war theory can explain their function in native societies very well. In spite of the absence of such theories to justify their actions, warfare among Native Americans, though often very brutal, normally did not result in many casualties. In his biography of the famous Indian warrior Crazy Horse, Larry McMurtry says: "Accustomed as we are to the wholesale slaughter of the two world wars, or even of the Civil War, it is hard to keep in mind that when Indian fought Indian a death count of more than three or four was unusual."[19] Just war rhetoric played a much more prominent role in the world wars and in the Civil War than it did in Native American war practice. But this does not seem to correlate in any specific way with the intensity of these wars.[20] I do not think, historically speaking, that wars fought with a high dose of moral discourse were in any measurable way better than those in which just war theories played only a minor role. Evidently, moral smartness does not bring about a more peaceful world than moral foolishness. If you think that your war is just, then this belief tends to make it easier for you to kill your enemy than when you think of it more in terms of a violent sports event.

Just war theorists like Michael Walzer imply that their moral smartness enables them to be impartial, that they are simply arguing on the basis of moral principles, and that they are able to apply these fairly and without bias. It seems to me, however, that something very different is actually happening. Just war theory seems to have the effect of disguising a bias as a just bias—and thus as a nonbias. It has the effect of making one's bias invisible to oneself. Just war theory operates on the illusion that war can be waged without bias, without selfish interests, and *only* for morally legitimate reasons with morally legitimate means. What its actual function seems to be is to provide the rhetoric for people or societies to deceive themselves into thinking that this is a realistic assumption.

In *Arguing about War* Walzer maintains that the "triumph of just war theory is clear enough." He refers to the examples of wars in Kosovo and Afghanistan, emphasizing that here, as well as in other contemporary wars, moral considerations to spare the life of civilians played a very important role (on the side of the just invaders, of course). He stipulates that just war theory may increasingly lead to a state of affairs in which "strategies are evaluated morally as well as militarily; that civilian deaths are minimized; that new technologies

are designed to avoid or limit collateral damage, and that these technologies are actually effective in achieving their intended purposes."[21] Walzer doesn't say that this is already the case, but he implies
that the "triumph of just war theory" has brought us much closer to
it. To me, this is not quite clear enough.

There are a number of present cases where huge military
machines fight against unjust terrorist resistance groups. Typically,
the military machines apply just war discourse to highlight their
moral difference from these terrorists by pointing out how much
they are concerned with sparing civilians while the terrorists openly
attack these innocent people. I am thinking here about the U.S.
and Israeli armies' operations against terrorists in Afghanistan, Iraq,
and Palestine. Obviously, the terrorists *do* target civilians. But it
seems clear enough (unfortunately it is difficult to obtain exact statistics and one has to rely on what one learns from the news) that
the civilian casualties caused by U.S. and Israeli operations (and,
more and more, from those carried out by private companies hired
by U.S. authorities) outnumber those caused by the terrorists. The
just warriors against terrorism, at least in these conflicts, actually
kill more civilians than the terrorists, and they do so, to use the
terms of Walzer's definition of terrorism, deliberately (the military is
perfectly aware that civilians will be killed in airstrikes) as well as
randomly (the target is, of course, not chosen randomly but that
doesn't make a difference to the random civilians who happen to be
around).[22]

This same paradoxical effect seems to be the result of the usage
of just weapons or, in Walzer's words, "new technologies ... designed
to avoid or limit collateral damage." In an article about Israeli military actions, Eyal Weizman says the following about so-called smart
bombs (which, in line with Walzer, could be called morally smart):
Their use has paradoxically "brought a higher level of civilian casualties, simply because the illusion of precision gives the military and
political complex the necessary justification to use explosives in
civilian environments. . . . In Gaza there have been two civilian
deaths for every intended killing during the al-Aqsa Intifada."[23]
Weizman's observation coincides with my suspicion that just war
theory, as it is actually applied, is not at all, in Walzer's own words, a
triumph that is clear enough.

Walzer's moral universe has very little to do with the realities of war. His ethical celebration of (morally) smart bombs is absurd. Smart bombs do not minimize civilian casualties. In fact they often increase those casualties, and they certainly played a role in the reversal of the ratio between enemy combatants and noncombatants killed in action. In past wars there were usually more soldiers killed than civilians. Partly as a result of the technology available to the U.S. military and its allies, enemy civilian casualties now typically outnumber friendly military casualties in the war on terrorism. Smart bombs are used in a terrorist manner according to Walzer's own definition of the deliberate and random killings of noncombatants. Their true purpose—not a hidden one but a most obvious one—is to minimize not enemy civilian deaths, but friendly military deaths. In fact, the extreme reduction in battle deaths in recent warfare is a result of military technology and has made soldiers on the ground and in battle more and more obsolete. This results in an extremely low death rate of "our troops" and makes valuable military targets practically out of reach for terrorists—which, ironically, leaves them with little else to attack other than civilians. Thus smart weapons not only increase the civilian casualty rate on the side of the enemy, but, indirectly, also contribute to its rise on the side of Israel and the Western countries that face terrorist attacks.

I am *not* trying to make a moral case for terrorism or against the United States and Israel—what I am saying is that Walzer's moral framework that describes terrorism as evil while depicting such wars as those fought by Israel against Palestinian terrorism or by the United States and their allies in Afghanistan and Iraq as just has little to do with the military reality of these conflicts. Walzer simply repeats a certain kind of moral rhetoric that has proliferated in the mass media and embellishes it with a little philosophical language. The logic of these conflicts and their impact on civilians cannot be adequately explained from a moral perspective. The war on terror does not really have a historical predecessor—it is a new phenomenon in the history of warfare. It follows a military logic that is intrinsically connected with current economic, political, geographic, technological, and other factors. To depict these wars in a moral fashion is nothing more than the telling of a fairy tale—and making smart bombs into moral weapons. These wars, and their weapons, are neither just nor unjust; they are the products of a complex social and technological evolution and deserve a much more subtle analysis than they receive in Walzer's ethical fiction.

I find it worrying that just war theorists like Walzer explicitly focus on the moral usage of the word just. This leads, I believe, to the problems outlined above. I am in favor of the separation of law and morality, and this applies to warfare as well. Given the important role that the mass media play in contemporary warfare, however, it is no surprise that the legal aspects of war receded to the background. Politicians and generals have to defend their wars on TV, and Hollywood movies focus on the moral aspects of wars, not on the legal ones. The image of a just/unjust war that is produced in the mass media is certainly the image of a primarily morally just/unjust war and not a legally just/unjust one. The mass media are much more inclined to communicate morally than legally. Given the social presence of the mass media nowadays, it is much more efficient to label a war morally just than to label it legally just. This is, I suggest, the reason why Walzer can speak of the triumph of just war theory. This triumph is in fact the triumph of moral over legal discourse about war in the mass media. It is not the triumph of a more humane kind of warfare, but of a specific rhetoric in the mass media.

Both George W. Bush and Tony Blair explicitly called the war in Iraq morally just and necessary—and this moral justification was depicted as more important than its legal justification. Contemporary U.S. warfare has violated a number of the legal norms of war as they are defined in the Geneva Convention. Bush and Blair's just war theory does not exactly match Walzer's, but they applied the rhetoric of a morally just war in order to conceal its legal injustice. Just war theory is a welcome tool for politicians, as well as for military and religious leaders, who intend to transform the legal terms *jus ad bellum* and *jus in bello* into moral terms and to tell on television a moral fairy tale about war. In a morally just war directed against what is declared an immeasurable evil anything goes. The laws of war can justly be ignored. A just war is a communicative construct that, in our society, is produced in the virtual morality of the mass media. Because of the carnivalistic aspects of this morality, however, it is no longer entirely convincing. Many of us do not believe in fairy tales anymore.

12 | ETHICS AND THE MASS MEDIA

NIKLAS LUHMANN BEGINS *The Reality of the Mass Media* with an apodictic overstatement: "Whatever we know about our society, or indeed about the world in which we live, we know through the mass media."[1] Of course, this is not true. We do not know, for instance, our parents through the mass media, and most of us who know how to cut the lawn did not learn how by watching TV or reading a book titled *Lawn Mowing for Dummies*. Luhmann uses the words "we" and "our" not in reference to us as single individuals, but to us as a society. All that *all* of us know about the world that we all *share*, we know through the mass media. We know about politics and sports, about movies and tomorrow's weather, about products and brands through the Internet, TV, the newspapers, and so on. Knowledge about politics, the weather, and brands is not individual knowledge, but general knowledge. It is knowledge that is supposed to be known in society. It is normally assumed that we know the name of the U.S. president and who Brad Pitt is—and even whether rain is predicted for the weekend. This is what constitutes our society, these are issues that we can assume that we can talk to anyone about. In Luhmann's words, these are the things that are "known to be known about."[2] There is no other source in society (not the church, not the schools) that provides all of us with this kind of general knowledge, or, ultimately, with the world that we know we all share. We do not share our parents or our backyard, but we do share the president, movie stars, and the weather.

We also share—in a very specific way that I explore in this chapter—morality and ethics, and we know about these, as Luhmann says, through the mass media as well. In our (Western) society what is seen as ours (in a general, and not individual sense) is made known only through the mass media, and this includes ethical knowledge. As individuals we may be taught about morality by our parents, in the church that we go to, in a class on the history of ethics at university—but we, as individuals, know that this specific morality (of, for instance, the Church of Latter-Day Saints or of Kant) is not necessarily the morality that is known to be known about. A significant number of individuals may believe that homosexuals should be given the death penalty or that slavery should be reinstated, but hardly anyone says this publicly because it is generally known that such views are considered unethical in our society. Neither a church, a school, nor a family can make ethics known to be known about in the same general and universal way that the mass media can. The mass media function as the medium of the mass *proliferation* of morality.[3] Here we are informed on a daily, indeed hourly, basis about what is considered morally appropriate and what is not—through the news, in the movies, and in advertisement.

One can see, for instance, that homosexuality is morally acceptable in our society, because politicians, even if they oppose gay marriage, express their love for their lesbian daughter and are praised for this in the mass media. We also see movies with gay cowboys as protagonists, and we see advertisements in which a gay couple is shown celebrating a special cell phone rate for partners. Whatever our parents, the Mormon church, or Kant tells us about the evils of homosexuality, it is obviously not really our morality in a general sense.

An attentive reader may think I have just contradicted myself. Above I stated that it was mainly for moral reasons that the majority of U.S. voters in various states did not approve of gay marriage. Did these voters not watch TV? Were they not aware that public morality had already accepted homosexuality? Of course they were. But the U.S. media presented the issue of gay marriage in such a way that a person, Vice President Dick Cheney being the perfect example, could well be opposed to gay marriage (and thus appear sympathetic to Christian fundamentalists) and still not be publicly exposed as homophobic and unethical. Such a position was morally sanctioned by the mass media. No one in the United States had to be ashamed to vote against gay marriage. The mass media had already justified the quite paradoxical attitude of having nothing against gays and lesbians while denying them the right to marry.

This example demonstrates a significant change in the sociology of ethics. In pre–mass media times our morality, in the general and universal sense, was largely proliferated by the church and, in connection with church teachings, the family. The Bible and other religious literature were the main sources of ethical values. This situation necessarily led to a relatively stable morality. The Bible remained more or less the same over centuries and although interpretations differed greatly, there were still significant limitations to both the scope and the speed of moral variation. It was simply impossible to produce and distribute a large number of texts, and the technical means to disseminate moral values universally—twenty-four hours a day, seven days a week—simply did not exist. In addition, there was also a strong tendency toward centralism in the Roman Catholic Church in Europe that allowed for the establishment of a more or less undisputed moral authority.

All this changed with the advent of the mass media, that is, the spread of printed matter (books and newspapers), then radio, film, and television, and now the Internet. With the emergence of the new mass media, public ethics became subject to variation and, in particular, increasingly accelerating change. News, advertisements, and entertainment programs change from minute to minute. They appear and disappear in a flash and have to be constantly renewed. This was (and is) obviously not the case with the Bible, and even papal communiqués appear only once in while. The speed with which the mass media constantly renew themselves means we must continuously refresh the knowledge that we get through them. We can't keep up with the news by reading a newspaper only once every six months. New movies and TV shows appear on a daily basis, and sports results become obsolete as quickly as the weather. If social morality is proliferated by the mass media as well, then ethics are now also subject to accelerated change and in need of constant renewal. The mass media are the fountain of youth for ethics in our society.[4]

The pope and the Catholic Church, as well as most other churches and religions, have great difficulty in altering their position on moral issues (the most famous with respect to the Catholic Church and many protestant churches in North America are currently abortion, contraception, and homosexuality). It is impossible for them to follow the speed of the mass media, even if they, as is the case in North America, constantly appear on television (televangelism) or the Internet. If they followed the speed of the mass media they would basically have to deny the sole authority of their respective holy scriptures and theological traditions. Churches tend to affirm that they derive their ethics from higher and eternal sources (just as Kant and other moral philosophers claim to derive their ethics from universal reason), and these do not lend themselves to much flexibility. Given the substantial sociological differences between the religious and the mass media production and reproduction of morality, it cannot be a surprise that these two moralities are out of sync. The churches cannot adapt to the speed with which the media change, and the media have no time to wait for the religions to move on. This is why the televangelists seem so much at odds with what we see when we switch channels to *Sex and the City*. The same is true, and, I believe, luckily so, for moral philosophy. Philosophical ethics have little chance of success in the age of mass media. It is quite unthinkable that what is known to be known about morality in society will be decided by *Critique of Practical Reason* alone instead of TV, movies, and the Internet.

In a paradoxical manner, televangelists do and do not, at the same time, partake of the mass media proliferation of morality. What they communicate is highly moral, but because of the typically uncompromising fundamentalism of their ethics they are immediately contradicted by the next program. While the fundamentalist televangelists claim to present an unambiguous and unequivocal ethics (nearly) all other programs on the mass media prove that our morality, in the general sense outlined above, is not at all unambiguous and unequivocal. It may well be thinkable that the mass media could be overtaken by and reduced to some sort of televangelism (as was probably the case under the Taliban regime in Afghanistan), but—luckily, I dare say—this is not the case at present with our mass media, and there seems to be little danger of it happening.

The we that is subject to the proliferation by the mass media is, as I emphasize once again, not the simple sum of individual moral beliefs and convictions. It is, rather, similar to public opinion—or, in former times, the so-called general will (*volonté générale*)—an impersonal and, most importantly, imprecise, nondefinable, and changing spectrum of what is considered acceptable in society. Our morality in this sense does not reflect *any* individual moral convictions; it rather serves as an ethical horizon of what is possible. This horizon includes some fundamentalist positions (like those of televangelists) but, paradoxically, at the same time excludes them, because they limit themselves to a radical corner within this horizon. Since this is the case they cannot be seen as truly representing our morality or public opinion. They are at the fringes of our morality and thus able to exert a certain moral influence, but, under the conditions of the contemporary mass media system, they are not in a position to define or determine it in the way they wish.

The fact that, unlike the Bible, the mass media texts, including news, entertainment, and advertising programs, disappear as soon as they have appeared and have to be replaced by *new* news, entertainment, and advertising programs, necessarily subjects our morality to constant change. It is not only, seen synchronically, a spectrum of significantly diverse and often contradictory views but also, seen diachronically, extremely unstable. An obvious example is sexual ethics. In the mass media products of the 1950s it is nearly impossible to find any homosexual couples or people who have children outside of marriage—and if one finds them they are typically presented as not in line with the morality of the time. (They may be presented sympathetically, but they are still moral outcasts.) This is obviously no longer the case. Homosexual partners or single mothers may still be presented as having social problems, but they are normally not depicted as morally deficient. And if they appear in situations where they are morally condemned, this condemnation is typically implicitly itself condemned as unethical. Today it is quite impossible in our mass media to produce a Hollywood movie that morally disapproves of homosexuality or single mothers.

It is also quite inconceivable that there will be, any time soon, a Hollywood movie that depicts child pornography or homosexual relations between adults and young teenagers as acceptable and ethically good (as was the case in ancient Greece). Similarly, it seems unlikely that polygamous marriage, once the norm in so many societies, will be presented as an example of moral excellence in a TV show.

Given the flexibility of the mass media system, it is, however, not predictable if (or when) things will change. There are no ethical foundations in the mass media that can prevent the possibility that the spectrum of our ethics may again approve of polygamy or sexual relationships between adults and teenagers. Similarly, there is no guarantee whatsoever that homosexuality or having children outside of marriage will not be morally condemned in the future. This may seem unlikely today, but our current sexual mass media ethics would have seemed quite unlikely in the 1950s.

Another important sociological aspect of the fact (and in my view this is indeed a fact) that the mass media have replaced the church and the family as the medium for *proliferating* morality in society is that it can no longer be said that the mass media are either the source of moral values (as, perhaps, churches and televangelists like to conceive of themselves) or, conversely, that they merely reflect public opinion (as liberal apologists of the mass media as the new forum of a civil society might like to see it). It is not the case that the construction of our ethics through the mass media is a simple one-way mechanism. The mass media are neither in the essentially active role of imposing morality on society nor in the merely passive role of giving a voice to the people as a mass megaphone. I think that neither of these two one-way models or simple cause-effect patterns is adequate for understanding how public morality is now constructed. This construction is instead a complex feedback process.

This feedback process is, I believe, somewhat similar to a propaganda mechanism that was envisioned by the great Chinese mass communicator Mao Zedong more than half a century ago:

In all the practical work of our party, all correct leadership is necessarily "from the masses to the masses." This means: take the ideas of the masses (scattered and unsystematic ideas) and concentrate them (through study turn them into concentrated and systematic ideas), then go to the masses and propagate and explain these ideas until the masses embrace them as their own, hold fast to them and translate them into action, and test the correctness of these ideas in such action, then once again concentrate ideas from the masses and once again go to the masses so that the ideas are persevered in and carried through. And so on, over and over again in endless spiral, with the ideas becoming more correct, more vital and richer each time.[5]

I have severe doubts, however, about any systematization of morality in the mass media. I don't believe that morality becomes more correct, more vital, and richer through them. The mass media are much more complex and much less hierarchical than a party, but, and I think this is the core of Mao's analysis, ethics in the mass media are produced from the masses to the masses, that is, not in a one-way direction, but as an autopoietic or self-producing and self-reproducing social process. The masses (namely, society) embrace these ethics as their own, translate them into practice, and then feed them back into the mass media over and over again in an endless spiral.

This means that ethics in the age of the mass media are neither totalitarian nor democratic (in a liberal sense). They are neither simply forced onto society nor are they simply derived from the people. In Luhmannian terms one may conceive of Mao's endless spiral as a mechanism of structural coupling. For sure, the mass media are not the party and society is not the people (or the masses), but mass media and society are connected in a feedback loop. The mass media literally *show* what is currently considered as morally good or bad in politics, religion, sports, the economy, medicine, and all other social systems. At the same time, these other systems watch the mass media and thus *see* what is ethical in society. The mass media enable all systems to irritate or perturb each other morally. Through the mass media, all social systems are continuously exposed to the spectrum of ethics in society and have to produce resonance to this. Through the mass media, the religious system becomes aware of changes in sexual ethics in the intimacy systems (people no longer marry before they have sex), for instance, and through the mass media, religion "reacts" to these changes (and makes pleas to preserve the traditional family). At the same time, politics becomes aware of the religious "reaction" to these changes and has to react itself (and come up with political opinions on how to deal with single mothers, for instance). I put "reaction" in quotation marks, because these systems do not, in a linear sequence, literally react. They rather reso-nate with each other simultaneously. It is not that what happens in one system precedes what happens in another system. All systems operate concurrently. This produces a complex feedback mecha-nism in which no single system (including the mass media system itself) is either the source or the recipient of morality. Mass media ethics, which are our ethics, are neither produced by any moral authority nor are they the result of a moral consensus among the people. They are an effect of the complex relations and the reso-nance between all social systems. The mass media are themselves one of these systems and at the same time a medium and a con-tributor to this effect. As a medium, they *accelerate* the social produc-tion of morality because of their incessant need for renewal. And they *proliferate* morality because of their global omnipresence. But they also take part in the shaping of morality. They do not objec-tively show the ethics of the other system, but they do show them on their own terms. As with every other system, the mass media have their own way of dealing with moral discourse, and thus they do not neutrally reflect the moral evaluations in the other systems but *select* what is interesting for them on the basis of their own functioning.

To once more make use of Niklas Luhmann's terminology, I highlight two of the main selection criteria of the mass media that, in my mind, significantly shape the character of contemporary eth-ics, namely conflict and scandal.[6]

Conflict seems to be of special interest to the mass media. When two countries are at war (be it hot or cold), this is more newsworthy than the harmonious relations between other countries. It is more interesting to hear that the United States and Canada disagree than that they agree. Similarly, most, if not all, entertainment programs focus on conflicts, be it between lovers, the police and criminals, the prosecution and the defense, or the Yankees and the Cardinals. These conflicts are, more often than not, at least in part, also moral con-flicts. Perhaps the main reason for the ambiguity of mass media morality is that the mass media are more interested in showing moral conflicts than in showing a moral consensus. This is true for both news and entertainment (and to a lesser extent for advertising). It is also not in the interest of mass media communication to resolve such conflicts because that would make it difficult to continue the programs. There is not, not even on FOX News, an absolute moral or political consensus, and there is no final moral solution shown in *Sex and the City*. While *individual* programs typically present clear-cut distinctions between goodies and baddies, the mass media *as a whole* do not.[7] There are quite a few movies in which the bad guys are more interesting than the good guys, (as well as video games such as *Grand Theft Auto*)—and even the good guys in movies are sometimes morally ambiguous (think of Clint Eastwood).

Televangelists, on the other hand, tend to come up with final (moral) evaluations—which makes them more similar to advertisement than to news or entertainment, and thus more *boring* than the latter. These preachers always advertise the same (moral) product and try to remove all possible doubt about its quality and the absolute inferiority of their competitors. Their moral monoculture makes them, for many, repetitive and thus tiring to watch.

The second selection criterion of the mass media that is immediately connected with their production of morality is scandal. What is scandalous is obviously more likely to be given airtime than what is not (and this is, again, the case for both news and entertainment programs). Scandals are moral norm violations. They are not necessarily violations of the law, but, and this is what makes them more interesting than mere legal missteps, highly ethically charged. One of the main media-morality scandals of the 1990s was the Clinton-Lewinsky affair. That the president had oral sex with a staff member in his office was not obviously illegal, but was, more than obviously, *scandalous* because of its moral implications. Even the fact that the president had lied was seen not as a mere legal issue, but as a moral outrage—of all people it was *the president* who lied.

The mass media are highly attracted by the scandalous, and this is due to the moral outrage that goes along with it. Scandals are exciting because they allow for a high dosage of morality. But this perhaps suggests that televangelism should also be considered very exciting. I think the important difference between the extreme focus on morality that scandals and televangelism share is that the former is *entertaining* whereas the latter is not. One can very well joke about the Clinton-Lewinsky scandal, but one is not really expected to joke about God. The scandalous, as opposed to the rigid morality of televangelism, is not fully serious; it is ambiguous, and often even ironic. It is, to use a term coined by Mikhail Bakhtin, "carnivalistic." Bakhtin derived the term from the European tradition of the carnival (in Italy) where, for a few days, people would make fun of the aristocrats and the clergy. The roles of the high and the low, of the respectful and the disrespected were reversed. In its comical farce, what was otherwise highly respected was subject to ridicule, and the low and the mean were elevated. Obviously, the morality of televangelism does not allow for such a carnival. You are not supposed to delight in the devil or to mock the Lord. Scandal, however, functions in a carnivalistic way: The president, the celebrity, the senator from Idaho, even the great moral televangelist himself becomes a laughingstock. The scandal exposes the ambiguity of morality, and it allows sinners to rejoice in the sins of the saints. Instead of reinforcing morality, it gives us an ironic break from ethics.

The scandalous is thus a mockery of morality; it is, in a sense, reversed morality. The outrage the media felt about Clinton did not reflect a genuine outrage about the immorality of the man. It was, rather, *fun* to see him morally exposed. I do not believe that, in our times of ambiguous sexual ethics, there was actual outrage about his actions. It was, instead, a carnivalistic outrage, a carnivalistic frenzy as a media spectacle. It was, as so many observers have commented, a *farce*. For the supporters of the president it was, of course, very unfortunate and politically lethal; nonetheless, it was a moral farce.

Scandal, in the guise of carnivalistic mass media morality, is a powerful tool. It can easily destroy its object socially; it can strip the powerful of their power, the rich of their money, and the priests of their frocks. But still, the scandal is always entertaining, otherwise it would not qualify as a scandal. The victims of scandal often try to diminish its effects by apologizing or offering excuses but this does not help much—it has already become a scandal. At the heart of the scandal is the fact that it is a mass media phenomenon, it is morality as an entertaining spectacle (one might think of shows like *Jerry Springer* or *Cheaters*), as carnivalism. It is morality not taken absolutely seriously; or it is ironic ethics, joyful outrage.

So what can be concluded from the intimate connection between the mass media and morality; what has happened to ethics in a world where eyes are glued to the screen? I think Luhmann was right in stating that all we know about the world (in the general sense outlined above) we know through the mass media, and in the same sense, all that we know about ethics we know through the mass media. In this way, the mass media can be seen as supermoral. There is no other system that is, on a social scale, so efficient in communicating morality. The mass media are the ideal stage for moral communication. Politicians like George W. Bush, among many others, understand this quite well. If they want to establish a good/evil distinction (in order to be identified with the good, of course), this can only happen through the mass media. All that we know about the axis of evil, we know through the mass media. At the same time, however, the mass media do not lend themselves to absolute moral judgments; they are oriented toward conflict, and this poses a great and, perhaps, insurmountable danger for moralistic politicians (and televangelists). Yes, we all know about the axis of evil through the mass media, and those who think that George Bush is good know this exactly from the same source. However, there are also a growing number of people nowadays (particularly in Europe and in the Middle East) who think they know that George Bush is not good, perhaps he is even evil, and they know this through the mass media as well. The moral power of the mass media may easily backfire on those who avail themselves of it.

The mass media do not control morality, they proliferate it—and they are inherently *amoral* themselves. For them, it does not matter what is considered moral or immoral. They are happy to present any morality as long as it is public morality. Mass media morality only works as nonfoundational, nonunequivocal, and nonstatic morality. This is not to say that anything goes in the mass media. The spectrum of the morally acceptable assuredly has its limits (child pornography, terrorism, and so on). There are many things that are not morally acceptable in the mass media. But these limits are subject to change and include a large degree of ambiguity. It is very likely that there will always be limits as long as there is mass media morality, but these limits are not stable or predictable.

Perhaps the most interesting, and, in my view, delightful aspect of mass media morality is its carnivalistic tendency. Mass media morality is without clear foundations, without strict rules, without any categorical imperative. It has a highly subversive power and does not lend itself to the establishment of a universal morality. It tends toward the scandalous, and the scandal is relentless entertainment without moral principle. This is what televangelists and George Bush have to live with. TV and the other media are their only moral playing field, but this field does not function in a way that allows them to dominate it. Similarly, moral philosophy will have to accept that public morality cannot be established in university classrooms or through academic publications. As long as all that we know about morality is known through the mass media, moral philosophers, religious fundamentalists, and political demagogues are not in a position bound for success.

I do not want to be misunderstood here. I am not suggesting that the mass media democratize ethics or that they lead to some sort of ethical progress. The morality of the mass media is a *virtual morality*; it does not correlate with the moral convictions of individual people; it does not give people a voice. It is rather an effect of a peculiar form of communication of a specific social system, namely the mass media. While the mass media proliferate morality on a global scale, they also subvert it. The mass media have no moral convictions; they are naturally amoral and intertwined in the endless, meaningless, and aimless spiral of superficial and contradictory moral communication. In this sense, the mass media function in a highly paradoxical and ambiguous way: While they flood society daily with moral discourse on a massive scale, they also constantly undermine the credibility of this very discourse. They maintain, spread, and accelerate moral communication but carnivalize and desubstantiate it at the same time. The mass media are, indeed, ethically rather foolish.

CONCLUSION | APPLIED AMORALITY

MY PURPOSE IN the conclusion is, first, to summarize my main arguments as concisely as I can. Second, I hope to avoid misunderstandings by pointing out once more what I have intended to say—and what I haven't.

Today, we live in a virtual world; everything that we know—"we" as all of us—we know not firsthand but through the mass media. This is also true for ethics. Ethics are, factually, virtual ethics. Morality is generally proliferated through the mass media; we learn about it primarily by looking at screens or paper. Morality is, therefore, a type of *communication* rather than something that is inherent in individuals or actions. Virtual morality as presented in the media is, on the one hand, very pervasive. It confronts us on a daily even hourly basis. On the other hand, it has become somewhat carnivalistic. There is no single or generally accepted moral paradigm. Morality is a monster with a thousand heads. You cut off one only for a dozen more to grow. Virtual ethics dominates, but it has no identity and is subject to constant change.

Morality is a form of communicative decomplexification. It simplifies things. For example, it simplifies war by guiding our weapons, by establishing a clear-cut distinction between those who can be killed and those who should not. It simplifies life by making us believe that we did what we did because it was morally the right thing to do. But reality is more complex than that. I firmly believe that even in cases where we have to make very difficult decisions in our life—for example, having an abortion, cheating on one's part-ner—we do not normally make these decisions on the basis of morality alone or come to primarily ethical resolutions. Life is too complex to be factually reduced to morality. We may well tell our-selves that what we do we do either in accord with or in violation of morality, but this is self-deception. What we believe to be the right thing is hardly ever the right thing for us in a *purely ethical* sense. And I do not see what is wrong with this. I do not see the benefit of reducing reality to morality.

In everyday situations there is even less need for pure morality. When we go to school or to work, when we listen to music or have a drink, when we cook or sleep, we are not in a moral mode. Life is not primarily moral. Even writing or reading this book is largely an amoral task. To reflect on morality is neither moral nor immoral. Yes, we live in a morally charged world of virtual ethics, but this does not mean that we live in a world of real ethics. One of the current paradoxes of morality is that it is at the same time so pervasive and so unessential: just as TV is on the whole.

There is, I believe, a certain danger in morality. Its tendency to simplify and polarize lends itself to being used as an effective tool in social conflicts. These can be violent or nonviolent. Typically, vio-lent conflicts, such as wars, go along with a high dose of moral com-munication. It is not the case that a relative lack of moral commu-nication is correlated with a society in relative disorder or that a surge in moral communication is correlated with a society in rela-tive peace. I also do not see how an increase in moral communica-tion has ever made the world, or a person, in any empirical sense "better."

Of course, morality is not only not good but also not evil. There is, from an amoral perspective, nothing that can be good or evil in an absolute sense. As Wittgenstein said in his "Lecture on Ethics," there is no "right way" to any place in the world.[1] The good way to London is the way that, for various reasons, we find good at a par-ticular time: it may be quick, comfortable, cheap, or have the most pleasant scenery. In the same sense there is no absolute justice or any other ethical value. We can use the terms "good" and "bad" in a more or less amoral sense. And in the same way we can call the use of moral communication good or bad. It is possible to say that the use of moral discourse is good or bad in this or that sense, without saying that morality is absolutely good or bad. In fact, one could say, following Wittgenstein, that the moral use of the words "good" and "evil" in an absolute sense represents a dangerous misuse of language. It implies that these terms have any absolute meaning when no such meaning is accessible. If you say that something is in an absolute sense good or evil you trick yourself into believing that you know something that cannot be known.

The function of morality in society, as Niklas Luhmann has said, is somewhat similar to the function of bacteria in the body. One should therefore be cautious with morality and "only touch it with the most sterile instruments and with gloves on" since it is a "highly contagious substance."[2] Bacteria are not good or bad in an absolute sense. They are a natural part and aspect of bodily functions, but they can be dangerous if they get out of hand. It is probably neither possible nor desirable to be a complete moral fool as envisioned by some Daoists. But I think it is quite possible, natural, and healthy to be an imperfect one, someone who, most of the time, does not really believe that she knows what is really good or bad, and who does not even use such terms in an absolute sense. We may not be able to live without moral bacteria, but we will be wise to keep them in check.

Since applied ethics are now so much in demand I end here with a concrete suggestion of how to apply the negative ethics of the moral fool: I demand that public broadcasts and performances that contain a high dose of morality—particularly certain Hollywood movies, TV shows, and news reports, and, especially, televised speeches and debates by politicians—must include a warning, like the ones we find on cigarette packs: "This product is full of morality and may therefore lead to unwanted communicative overengagement, possibly resulting in damage to both personal and social health." At the very least, to protect minors, there should be a rating system that indicates to parents how morally polluted each program is. For all televangelist broadcasts I suggest a rating of HE (highly ethical), a rating that makes viewing such a broadcast illegal for all those not yet of legal drinking age.

NOTES

Introduction

1. Niklas Luhmann has posed this very question both implicitly and explicitly in his many criticisms of morality. See, for instance, "The Sociology of the Moral and Ethics," *International Sociology* 11.1 (March 1996): 27–36.

2. First published as "Wittgenstein's Lecture on Ethics," *Philosophical Review* 74 (1965): 3–12. The lecture was probably delivered at Cambridge University in 1929 or 1930.

3. Wittgenstein discusses the moral distinction of good/evil in connection with the epistemological (or even ontological) distinction right/wrong (or true/false). I agree with Wittgenstein's view that absolute judgments are impossible with respect to any of these distinctions, but my argumentation in this book is largely confined to moral issues.

4. G. W. F. Hegel, *Hegel's Aesthetics: Lectures on Fine Art*, trans. T. M. Knox (Oxford: Oxford University Press, 1975), 1:464.

5. See my discussion in chapter 2 of the distinction between ethics and morality.

6. Walter Kaufmann, "Hegel's Ideas about Tragedy," in *New Studies in Hegel's Philosophy*, ed. W. E. Steinkraus (New York: Holt, Rinehart and Winston, 1971), 202.

7. I thoroughly disagree with Hegel's quite sexist analysis of *Sittlichkeit* and *Moral* in the *Phenomenology of Spirit*, where he states: "Nature, not the accident of circumstances or choice, assigns one sex to one law, the other to the other law" (G. W. F. Hegel, *Phenomenology of Spirit*, trans. A. V. Miller [Oxford: Oxford University Press, 1977], 280).

8. *Analects* 13.18. Quoted in Roger T. Ames and Henry Rosemont Jr., *The Analects of Confucius: A Philosophical Translation* (New York: Ballantine, 1998), 167.

9. This is a somewhat provocative proposition since the Confucians are normally understood as moralist philosophers, particularly by their amoral Daoist critics. My understanding of Confucius, however, is a little more complex. I believe that Confucian morality is based on nonmoral, emotional cultivation. The Confucians *are* moralists, but their morality is based on amoral and natural feelings.

10. *Analects* 1.2. In Ames and Rosemont, *Analects of Confucius*, 71.

11. "Latimer Should Be Granted Clemency," *Globe and Mail*, Saturday, 8 December 2007, A28.

12. See Niklas Luhmann, *Law as a Social System*, trans. Klaus A. Ziegert (Oxford: Oxford University Press, 2004).

13. This expression alludes to the language used in advertising, such as, Miller Lite and Bud Light.

14. Richard Rorty, "Solidarity and Objectivity," in *Post-Analytic Philosophy*, ed. John Rajchman and Cornel West (New York: Columbia University Press, 1985), 3–19.

1. The Moral Fool

1. For an English translation see Lin Yutang, *The Importance of Understanding (Translations from the Chinese)* (Cleveland: Forum Books, World Publishing, 1963), 385. I comment on this allegory in detail in *The Philosophy of the Daodejing* (New York: Columbia University Press, 2006), 99 ff.

2. Robert C. Solomon, *In the Spirit of Hegel* (New York, Oxford: Oxford University Press, 1983), 534–35; emphasis in the original.

3. Charles Taylor, *Hegel* (Cambridge: Cambridge University Press, 1975), 376.

4. Niklas Luhmann, *Paradigm Lost: Über die ethische Reflexion der Moral: Rede anläßlich der Verleihung des Hegel-Preises, 1989* (Frankfurt/Main: Suhrkamp, 1990), 19.

5. Drucilla Cornell, *The Philosophy of the Limit* (New York: Routledge, 1992), 13. For a discussion of this quote, see William Rasch, "Immanent Systems, Transcendental Temptations, and the Limits of Ethics," in *Observing Complexity: Systems Theory and Postmodernity*, ed. William Rasch and Cary Wolfe (Minneapolis: University of Minnesota Press, 2000), 73–98.

6. Nietzsche introduces the term "extra-moral" in his early treatise *Über Wahrheit und Lüge im aussermoralischen Sinne* (On Truth and Lying in an Extra-Moral Sense). I prefer to use the more common English term "amoral." Nevertheless, this book is highly influenced by the criticisms of morality found throughout Nietzsche's whole oeuvre. I appreciate Nietzsche's diagnosis of the pathology of morality, but sometimes this very diagnosis seems to be quite pathological as well, particularly when he explicitly defends an *im*moral position, that is to say, a merely inverted morality, as was true in "Morality as the Enemy of Nature," in *Twilight of the Idols*. However, as was so often the case, Nietzsche was ahead of his time in pointing out the semiotic character of morality, that is to say, its communicative aspects. My own analysis of morality in this book fully concurs with the following observations found in "The 'Improvers' of Mankind," in *Twilight of the Idols*, namely, "there are no such things as moral facts" and "morality is only an interpretation of certain phenomena: or, more strictly speaking, a misinterpretation of them. . . . Morality is

merely a sign language" (Friedrich Wilhelm Nietzsche, *Twilight of the Idols, with the Antichrist and Ecce Homo*, trans. Anthony M. Ludovici [Hertfordshire: Wordsworth, 2007], 37).

2. Negative Ethics

1. Hans Saner, "Formen der negativen Ethik: Eine Replik," in *Negative Ethik*, ed. Henning Ottmann (Berlin: Parerga, 2005), 27–30.
2. Angus C. Graham, *Chuang-Tzu: The Inner Chapters* (Indianapolis: Hackett, 2001), 147. See *Zhuangzi jijie*, in *Zhuzi jicheng* (Peking: Zhonghua, 1954), 3:255, for the original. Transliteration altered.
3. Graham, *Chuang-Tzu,* 201–2. See *Zhuangzi jijie*, 3:55, for the original.
4. Nietzsche lists this confusion as the first of the "four great errors" in the so-called section.
5. Graham, *Chuang-Tzu*, 211. See *Zhuangzi jijie*, 3:165–66, for the original.
6. Graham, *Chuang-Tzu*, 211. See *Zhuangzi jijie*, 3:166, for the original.
7. Graham, *Chuang-Tzu*, 213. See *Zhuangzi jijie*, 3:171, for the original.
8. Graham, *Chuang-Tzu*, 90. See *Zhuangzi jijie*, 3:109, for the original.
9. Graham, *Chuang-Tzu*, 129. See *Zhuangzi jijie*, 3:229, for the original.
10. Graham, *Chuang-Tzu*, 207–8. See *Zhuangzi jijie*, 3:156–57, for the original.
11. Graham, *Chuang-Tzu*, 208. See *Zhuangzi jijie*, 3:157–58, for the original.
12. Graham, *Chuang-Tzu*, 174. See *Zhuangzi jijie*, 3:199, for the original.
13. For an antihumanist reading of the *Lao zi*, see Hans-Georg Moeller, *The Philosophy of the Daodejing* (New York: Columbia University Press, 2006).
14. I have in mind authors such as N. Katherine Hayles and Donna J. Haraway.
15. John Gray, *Straw Dogs: Thoughts on Humans and Other Animals* (London: Granta, 2002), xiii.
16. Ibid., 32.
17. Ibid., 88.
18. Ibid., 96.
19. Ibid., 116
20. Ibid., 112.

3. The Redundancy of Ethics

1. Angus C. Graham, *Chuang-Tzu: The Inner Chapters* (Indianapolis: Hackett, 2001), 81. See *Zhuangzi jijie*, in *Zhuzi jicheng* (Peking: Zhonghua, 1954), 3:351, for the original.
2. Niklas Luhmann, *The Reality of the Mass Media* (Stanford: Stanford University Press, 2000), 79.

3. See the introduction for a more detailed discussion of how I use the terms "love" and "law" in this book.

4. See section V.B.b. in G. W. F. Hegel, *Phenomenology of Spirit*, trans. A. V. Miller (Oxford: Oxford University Press, 1977).

5. On the issue of legal coherence, see Niklas Luhmann, *Law as a Social System* (Oxford: Oxford University Press, 2005).

6. Niklas Luhmann, *Gibt es in unserer Gesellschaft noch unverzichtbare Normen?* (Heidelberg: C. F. Müller Juristischer Verlag, 1993), 19; my translation.

4. The "Morality of Anger"

1. Walter Berns, *For Capital Punishment: Crime and the Morality of the Death Penalty* (New York: Basic Books, 1979). See in particular chapter 5, "The Morality of Capital Punishment." The excerpt from this book included in *Philosophy of Punishment*, ed. Robert M. Baird and Stuart E. Rosenbaum (Buffalo: Prometheus Books, 1988) 85–93, is titled "The Morality of Anger."

2. Berns, *For Capital Punishment*, 154–56.

3. Ibid., 8.

4. From "The Morality of Anger," in *Philosophy of Punishment*, 86. This reference to Aristotle is not included in the original book.

5. *Rhetorica*, 1378a, quoted in Aristotle, *On Rhetoric: A Theory of Civic Discourse*, trans. George A. Kennedy (New York Oxford University Press, 1991), 124.

6. Ibid., 1378b, in Kennedy's translation of *On Rhetoric*, 125.

7. Ibid., 1380a, in Kennedy's translation of *On Rhetoric*, 130–31.

8. Ibid., in Kennedy's translation of *On Rhetoric*, 130.

9. For contemporary Zen Buddhist philosophy and its negative ethics see the works of Masao Abe, particularly *Zen and Western Thought* (Honolulu: University of Hawaii Press, 1985), as well as Abe's contributions in *The Emptying God:. A Buddhist-Jewish-Christian Conversation*, ed. John B. Cobb, Jr. and Christopher Ives (Maryknoll, N.Y.: Orbis, 1990).

10. Quite prominently, for instance, in Dōgen's *Shōbōgenzō*. See *The Heart of Dōgen's Shōbōgenzō*, trans. Norman Wadell and Masao Abe (Albany: State University of New York Press, 2002), 3. William F. Powell lists a number of occurrences of the same phrase in his translation of *The Record of Tung-shan* (Honolulu: University of Hawaii Press, 1986), 78–79n. 89 and 41.

11. John Blofeld, *The Zen Teaching of Hui Hai on Sudden Illumination* (London: Rider, 1962), 50. The English word "love" in this translation is somewhat problematic. It does not really mean passionate, romantic, or unconditional love, nor does it mean love in the sense of affection—as I use it in this book. Love here means the opposite of aversion, and thus something akin to liking or attraction.

12. Ibid., 54, 60.

13. Ibid., 74, 137.

14. *The Zen Teachings of Master Lin-chi*, trans. Burton Watson (Boston: Shambhala, 1993), 61.

15. Ibid., 53.

5. Ethics and Aesthetics

1. Burton Watson, *The Complete Works of Chuang Tzu* (New York: Columbia University Press, 1968), 89. See *Zhuangzi yinde* (Peking 1947), 18/6/82–19/6/86.

2. Richard Rorty, "Analytic Philosophy and Conversational Philosophy," typescript, 6.

3. Richard Rorty, *Contingency, Irony, and Solidarity* (Cambridge: Cambridge University Press, 1989), 145.

4. Ibid., 141.

5. I discuss the issue of "good baddies" and explain the term "carnivalistic" in chapter 12.

6. The Presumptions of Philosophical Ethics

1. Niklas Luhmann, *Paradigm Lost: Über die ethische Reflexion der Moral: Rede anläßlich der Verleihung des Hegel-Preises, 1989* (Frankfurt/Main: Suhrkamp, 1990), 21.

2. Niklas Luhmann, "Politik, Demokratie, Moral" in *Normen, Ethik und Gesellschaft, Konferenz der Deutschen Akademie der Wissenschaften*, (Mainz: Philipp von Zabern. 1977), 17.

3. Immanuel Kant, *Grounding for the Metaphysics of Morals*, trans. James W. Ellington (Indianapolis: Hackett, 1981), 1.

4. Ibid., 2.

5. Ibid., 3.

6. Ibid.

7. G. W. F. Hegel, *Phenomenology of Spirit*, trans. A.V. Miller (Oxford: Oxford University Press, 1977), 262.

8. Immanuel Kant, *The Metaphysics of Morals*, trans. Mary Gregor (Cambridge: Cambridge University Press, 1991), 96; emphasis in the original.

9. Ibid., 101; emphasis in the original.

10. "We punish criminals principally in order to pay them back, and we execute the worst of them out of moral necessity," says Walter Berns, in a very Kantian fashion, in Berns, *For Capital Punishment: Crime and the Morality of the Death Penalty* (New York: Basic Books, 1979), 8.

11. Kant, *The Metaphysics of Morals*, 142–43.

12. Ibid., 144–45.

13. *The Zen Teachings of Master Lin-chi*, trans. Burton Watson (Boston: Shambhala, 1993), 61.

14. Jeremy Bentham, *An Introduction to the Principles of Morals and Legislation* (Oxford: Clarendon Press, 1996), 11; emphasis in the original.

15. Ibid., 54.

16. Ibid., 64.

17. F. Rosen, introduction in Bentham, *An Introduction to the Principles of Morals and Legislation*, xli.

18. "Wittgenstein's Lecture on Ethics" *Philosophical Review* 74 (1965): 3–12.

7. The Myth of Moral Progress

1. A much more elaborate—but similar in content—deconstruction of this aspect of the myth of moral progress is the chapter "Non-Progress" in John Gray, *Straw Dogs: Thoughts on Humans and Other Animals* (London: Granta, 2002), 153–89.

2. Lawrence Kohlberg, *Essays on Moral Development*, vol. 1, *The Philosophy of Moral Development: Moral Stages and the Idea of Justice* (San Francisco: Harper and Row, 1981).

3. Throughout this paragraph I quote from the appendix in Kohlberg, *The Philosophy of Moral Development*, 409–12.

4. Lawrence Kohlberg and Mordecai Nisan, "Cultural Universality of Moral Judgment Stages: A Longitudinal Study in Turkey" in Kohlberg, *Essays on Moral Development*, vol. 2, *The Psychology of Moral Development: The Nature and Validity of Moral Stages* (San Francisco: Harper and Row, 1984), 582.

5. Lawrence Kohlberg and Anne Colby, *The Measurement of Moral Judgment*, 2 vols. (Cambridge: Cambridge University Press, 1987).

6. Kohlberg admits that there are cultural factors that influence the results of his surveys, but he still maintains that the model is universally valid. See the two cross-cultural studies in Kohlberg, *The Psychology of Moral Development:* Kohlberg and Nisan, "Cultural Universality of Moral Judgment Stages: A Longitudinal Study in Turkey," 582–593, and Lawrence Kohlberg, John Snarey, and Joseph Reimer, "Cultural Universality of Moral Judgment Stages: A Longitudinal Study in Israel." 594–620.

7. Kohlberg, *The Philosophy of Moral Development*, 412.

8. Such attempts have been made. See Heiner Roetz, *Die chinesische Ethik der Achsenzeit* (Frankfurt/Main: Suhrkamp, 1992). Roetz's attempt to discover Kohlberg's sixth stage and his rational moral universals in Confucianism is in my view perfectly analogous to and equally as absurd as earlier attempts by Christian missionaries to discover Christian universal values and beliefs. I do not think that Confucianism is in need of Christian or Kohlbergian missionaries.

9. Kohlberg, *The Philosophy of Moral Development*, 142. See also, Kohlberg, Snarey, and Reimer, "Cultural Universality of Moral Judgment Stages: A Longitudinal Study in Israel," in Kohlberg, *The Psychology of Moral Development*, 594–620.

10. A. S. Neill, *Summerhill School: A New View of Childhood* (New York: St. Martin's Press, 1993), 44.

11. See, for example, chapters 10 and 55 in the *Daodejing*.

12. For more information on the image of the infant, see "The Body (of Infants and Corpses)" in my *Daoism Explained: From the Dream of the Butterfly to the Fishnet Allegory (Ideas Explained)* (Chicago: Open Court, 2004), 74–81.

8. For the Separation of Morality and Law

1. Rasch, Nobles, and Schiff work with Niklas Luhmann's social systems theory. Rasch argues against the subjection of the legal system to moral oversight saying that the "'ethical moment' threatens to become, then, the moment that jeopardizes the autonomous self-reproduction of the system by dissolving the clear distinction between system and environment. The law ceases to be the law when the ethically occupied other lays it down. It becomes a commandment" (William Rasch, *Niklas Luhmann's Modernity. The Paradoxes of Differentiation* [Stanford: Stanford University Press, 2000], 143). Nobles and Schiff describe in detail the history of the separation of law and morality and trace it back to the seventeenth century. Referring to Hobbes they write: "To an external observer, the legal system's claim to be applying moral principles could appear quite bogus" (Richard Nobles and David Schiff, *A Sociology of Jurisprudence* [Oxford: Hart, 2006]), 63.

2. This is how I read section C.C.c ("Reason as Testing Laws") in the *Phenomenology of Spirit*. See G.. W. F. Hegel, *Phenomenology of Spirit*, trans. A. V. Miller (Oxford: Oxford University Press, 1977), 256–62.

3. Niklas Luhmann, "Politicians, Honesty, and the Higher Amorality of Politics," *Theory, Culture, and Society* 11 (1994): 25–36.

4. Niklas Luhmann, *Law as a Social System*, trans. Klaus A. Ziegert (Oxford: Oxford University Press, 2005), 445, 214–15.

5. Ibid., 460.

6. Martha Nussbaum, *Sex and Social Justice* (New York: Oxford University Press, 1998), 87.

7. Ibid.

8. Niklas Luhmann, *Die Gesellschaft der Gesellschaft* (Frankfurt/Main: Suhrkamp, 1997), 1022.

9. Richard Rorty, "Human Rights, Rationality, and Emotions" in *On Human Rights: The Oxford Amnesty Lectures, 1993*, ed. Stephen Shute and Susan Hurley (New York: Basic Books, 1993).

9. Morality and Civil Rights

1. Quoted in Nelson Manfred Blake, *A History of American Life and Thought* (New York: McGraw-Hill, 1963), 124; emphasis in original.

10. How to Get a Death Verdict

1. There was some sort of makeshift tribunal but it did not meet contemporary legal standards.

2. I am not singling out the United States as the worst country that still practices the death penalty. I am simply not as familiar with the practice in other countries and thus do not know if or to what extent my analysis of the situation in the United States also applies to them.

3. See "Appendix B: Reported Frequencies of National Death Penalty Policy, 1980 to 2001," in Franklin E. Zimring, *The Contradictions of American Capital Punishment* (Oxford: Oxford University Press, 2003).

4. As with virtually all fundamental human rights, there is no consensus, neither diachronically nor synchronically, about the right to life. The European Convention on Human Rights as adopted in 1950 explicitly declares the death penalty to be in line with this supposed right, whereas an amendment to it commissioned in 1982 requires the abolition of the death penalty (Zimring, *Contradictions of American Capital Punishment*, 28–29). The abolition of the death penalty in Europe is certainly often seen as a result of the acceptance of human rights, but it can hardly be called an effect of (often ineffective and legally ambiguous) human rights declarations. I would argue that the relatively recent European development of declaring the death penalty a violation of human rights is not so much a reason for the actual abolishment of the death penalty as it is that the increasing contradiction between death penalty practice and functionally differentiated law resulted either in practical or explicit abolition in many European countries. This historical trend is, in my view, the reason for the recent European construction of the death penalty as a human rights violation. There is no objective human right that would make the death penalty inherently illegal. The popularity of human rights semantics made it convenient to justify the abolition of the death penalty on its basis. It was a semantics that came in handy when the death penalty became socially obsolete. The idea that human rights are at odds with the death penalty is not a cause but an important side effect of the global trend toward abolition.

5. See the section on Kant in this chapter.

6. Phoebe C. Ellsworth and Samuel Gross, "Hardening of the Attitudes: Americans' Views on the Death Penalty, " in *The Death Penalty in America: Current Controversies*, ed. Hugo Adam Bedau (New York: Oxford University Press, 1997), 90–115; William C. Bailey and Ruth D. Peterson, "Murder, Capital Punishment, and Deter-

rence: A Review of the Literature," in *The Death Penalty in America*,, 138; Ernest van den Haag, "The Death Penalty Once More," in *The Death Penalty in America*, 449–50; Richard C. Dieter, "Millions Misspent: What Politicians Don't Say about the High Costs of the Death Penalty," in *The Death Penalty in America*, 402.

7. Stuart Banner, *The Death Penalty: An American History* (Cambridge, Mass.: Harvard University Press, 2002), 311.

8. This is obviously closely related to the American morality of anger discussed in chapter 4.

9. See, for instance, van den Haag, "The Death Penalty Once More," in *The Death Penalty in America*, 445–56; Tom Sorell, *Moral Theory and Capital Punishment* (Oxford: Basil Blackway, Open University, 1987).

10. Immanuel Kant, *The Metaphysics of Morals*, trans. Mary Gregor (Cambridge: Cambridge University Press, 1991), 143.

11. See, in particular, Sorell, *Moral Theory and Capital Punishment*, 30–32, 162.

12. For Kant's discussion of these issues see Mary Gregor's translation of *The Metaphysics of Morals*, 140–45.

13. Günter Wohlfart made me aware of the surprising parallels between Kant's and Robespierre's moral philosophies. See his book *Die Kunst des Lebens und andere Künste: Skurrile Skizzen zu einem euro-daoistischen Ethos ohne Moral* (Berlin: Parerga, 2005), 75–76.

14. Maximilien Robespierre, *Virtue and Terror*, ed. Slavoj Žižek, trans. John Howe (London: Verso, 2007), 126, 137.

15. Ibid., 132–33.

16. Immanuel Kant, "On the Common Saying: 'This May Be True in Theory, but It Does Not Apply in Practice,'" in *Kant's Political Writings*, ed. H. Reiss, trans. H. B. Nisbet (Cambridge: Cambridge University Press. 1970), 81, 63. Ironically, in the speech in which Robespierre vehemently demands the execution of the king, he also presents himself as a death penalty abolitionist who "abhor[s] the death penalty generously prescribed by your laws" (ibid., 64). It seems that soon after he rectified his moral principles.

17. See van den Haag and Bern quotations in this chapter.

18. "Every murderer—anyone who commits murder, orders it, or is an accomplice in it—must suffer death" (Kant, *The Metaphysics of Morals*, 143).

19. Sorell, *Moral Theory and Capital Punishment*, 4.

20. Walter Berns, "The Morality of Anger," in *Philosophy of Punishment*, ed. Robert M. Baird and Stuart E. Rosenbaum (Buffalo: Prometheus Books, 1988), 89; van den Haag, "The Death Penalty Once More," in *The Death Penalty in America*, 451–52; Banner, *The Death Penalty*, 282.

21. Herbert Morris, "Person and Punishment," in *Philosophy of Punishment*, 78; van den Haag, "The Death Penalty Once More, " in *The Death Penalty in America*, 454.

22. Hugo Adam Bedau, "Innocence and the Death Penalty: Assessing the Danger of Mistaken Executions," in *The Death Penalty in America*, 344–60.

23. Jessica Blank and Eric Jensen, *The Exonerated* (New York: Dramatists Play Service, 2004), 5. The death penalty was declared unconstitutional by the U.S. Supreme Court in 1973 ; it was reinstated in 1976.

24. Zimring, *Contradictions of American Capital Punishment*, 42–64.

25. Ibid., 51–52.

26. Ibid., 55.

27. Ibid., 57.

28. The need for this term is closely related to the morality of anger discussed in chapter 4.

29. Zimring, *Contradictions of American Capital Punishment*, 58, 61.

30. Ibid., 59

31. Ibid., 62.

32. Berns, "The Morality of Anger," in *Philosophy of Punishment*, 89.

33. Joseph L. Hoffman, "How American Juries Decide Death Penalty Cases: The Capital Jury Project," in *The Death Penalty in America*, 335.

34. Ibid.

35. Quoted in Zimring, *Contradictions of American Capital Punishment*, 54; bracketed material in the original.

36. Ibid., 55; emphasis in the original.

37. Hoffman, "How American Juries Decide Death Penalty Cases," in *The Death Penalty in America*, 338; emphasis in the original.

38. Ibid.

39. Ibid., 333.

40. Blank and Jensen, *The Exonerated*, 5.

41. Ibid., 34.

42. Bedau, "Background and Developments," in *The Death Penalty in America*, 19. Detailed statistics are found on p. 20.

43. Banner, *The Death Penalty*, 276.

44. Quoted in Zimring, *Contradictions of American Capital Punishment*, 61.

45. Niccolò Machiavelli, *The Prince*, trans. George Bull (London: Penguin, 2003), 53.

46. Larry Myers, "An Appeal for Clemency: The Case of Harold Lamont Otey," in *The Death Penalty in America*, 361–83; quotes are on 381 and 383.

47. Kant, *The Metaphysics of Morals*, 146.

11. Masters of War

1. I particularly recommend *Sun-tzu: The Art of Warfare*, trans. Roger T. Ames (New York: Ballantine, 1993).

2. Moral reflections on warfare that discuss the conditions for legitimate wars exist in

other schools of ancient Chinese philosophy, particularly in Confucianism (Mencius) and Mohism.

3. For other significant differences see the chapter on war in my *Philosophy of the Daodejing* (New York: Columbia University Press, 2006), 75–86. Daoist war philosophy is not only amoral but also nonheroic and unconcerned with ethnic or national issues.

4. An interesting exception is Heraclitus. Often, the pre-Socratics, in particular Heraclitus, are surprisingly similar to Daoist positions. Günter Wohlfart has investigated this issue repeatedly. See, for instance, chapter 8, on Heraclitus and Laozi, in his book *Der Philosophische Daoismus* (Cologne: Chora, 2001).

5. Michael Walzer, *Just and Unjust Wars: A Moral Argument with Historical Illustrations* (New York: Basic Books, 1977), xii–xv.

6. Ibid., 253, 259, 263.

7. Ibid., 101.

8. Ibid., 106.

9. Ibid., 85.

10. Ibid., 10.

11. Jean Bethke Elshtain, "Epilogue: Continuing Implications of the Just War Tradition," in *Just War Theory*, ed. Jean Bethke Elshtain (New York: New York University Press, 1992), 324.

12. Robert L. Holmes, "Can War Be Morally Justified? The Just War Theory," in *Just War Theory*, 220; emphasis in the original.

13. Following a suggestion by John Maraldo, I note that I indeed do refer here generally to all academic so-called just war principles, including the principle of double effect, that is the idea that some bad things are ethically allowed (particularly in war) as long as they fulfil a number of good conditions. Walzer's arguments referred to above are examples of how this principle can be applied.

14. Michael Walzer, *Arguing about War* (New Haven: Yale University Press, 2004).

15. Ibid., 130–31.

16. Ibid., 85–98.

17. *The World Almanac and Book of Facts, 1998,* 959. It is interesting to compare the relative death toll of Americans in the 1991 Iraq war with U.S. wars in the past century. The relative death toll in Vietnam and Korea was about ten times higher (0.66 percent and 0.64 percent, respectively) and the likelihood of dying in World War I and II was more than forty times higher (2.46 percent and 2.49 percent, respectively) (ibid., 161).

18. According to *The World Almanac and Book of Facts, 1998,* there were over 85,000 Iraqi casualties (776). It is unclear how many of these were fatal. I do not think that a death toll of 30,000 Iraqis is an overestimate. Most terrorist acts (except such major ones as the 9/11 attack) have less effective ratios of loss.

19. Larry McMurtry, *Crazy Horse* (New York: Viking, 1999), 95.

20. The weaponry used in the world wars and in the Civil War was much more power-ful than that used by Native Americans, which leads to a much higher casualty rate. Still, it seems obvious that the focus on killing the enemy was much more preva-lent in these Western wars than it typically was in Indian warfare.

21. Walzer, *Arguing about War*, 11–12.

22. On the very day that I wrote this (28 October 2007) I watched a news program on CBS. A highly ranked military officer who fought during the second war against Iraq explained in an interview that the number of acceptable civilian deaths in attacking an important target (such as Saddam Hussein and other leaders) was twenty-nine. If thirty or more civilians were likely to die, the strike had to be authorized by the U.S. president or other eminent authorities. The officer stated that in such attacks probably more than two hundred civilians were killed during his time of service—but none of the actual targets. The same news program showed an interview with the Afghan president Hamid Karzai demanding that the U.S. army cease its practice of airstrikes against Afghan villages. So many civilians have been killed that, according to the news report, the U.S. army is even more resented by the population than the Soviet army was during its occupation.

23. Eyal Weizman, "Walking through Walls: Soldiers as Architects in the Israeli-Palestinian Conflict," *Radical Philosophy* 136 (March–April 2006): 16.

12. Ethics and the Mass Media

1. Niklas Luhmann, *The Reality of the Mass Media* (Stanford: Stanford University Press, 2000), 1.

2. Ibid., 20.

3. It should be stressed here that while I think it is very obvious that the mass media function in society, that is, *sociologically*, as the means of the proliferation of ethics, I still think that the *aesthetic* value of mass media art (such as films and books) has no specific relation to its moral content. Most movies shown on TV, in the theaters, or downloaded from the Internet contribute to the proliferation of morality in our society. But I think that what makes a good film an aesthetically good film (or a good novel an aesthetically good novel) can by no means be induced from its moral message (see chapter 5). Books and films have the sociological effect of pro-liferating morality, but their aesthetic value does not correlate with this effect. The aesthetic value of a mass media product should not be confused with its function in society.

4. See Luhmann, *The Reality of the Mass Media*, 80, for a similar observation.

5. This quotation is taken from a text called "Some Questions of Leadership" (*Guanyu lingdao fangfa de ruogan wenti*). According to the official edition of Mao Zedong's *Selected Works*, it was presented to the Central Committee of the Chinese Communist Party on 1 June 1943. The Chinese version is included in *Mao Zedong*

xuan ji (Peking: Renmin, 1951–61), 3:854. The English translation here follows Stuart R. Schram, *The Political Thought of Mao Tse-tung*, rev. and enl. ed. (New York: Praeger, 1969), 316–17. An English translation of the whole text is included in Mao Zedong, *Selected Works* (Peking: Foreign Languages Press, 1964), 3:117–22.

6. See Luhmann, *The Reality of the Mass Media*, 28–29.

7. See chapter 5 for a discussion of goodies and baddies.

Conclusion

1. See the introduction for more about Wittgenstein's lecture.

2. Niklas Luhmann, "Ethik als Reflexionstheorie der Moral," in Luhmann, *Gesellschaftsstruktur und Semantik: Studien zur Wissenssoziologie der modernen Gesellschaft, Band 3* (Frankfurt/Main: Suhrkamp, 1993), 359.

INDEX

Bible, 109–10
Bin Laden, Osama, 35, 118
Blair, Tony, 171
Blofeld, John, 60, 192n11
Buddhists: Western philosophers and
    Daoists v., 57; *see also* Zen Buddhism
Bush, George H., 154
Bush, George W., 171, 182, 183

Calmness, 56, 61
Canada, 84, 135
Capital punishment; *see* Death penalty
Carnivalistic outrage, 181
Categorical imperative, 81–82
Categories of opposites, 58
Catholic Church, 175; *see also* Christian
    morality
CBS News, 200n22
Cervantes, Miguel de, 68
Character judgment, 23
Cheaters, 181
Cheating spouse, 48–50, 112–13, 186
Children: Kant on "illegitimate,"
    84–85; kibbutz for, 100; moral
    communication improving with age,
    90, 94–98, 102; parental love for, 8;
    Summerhill school, 100–1; *see also*
    Kohlberg, Lawrence
China, 38, 135, 157; *see also* Mao Zedong
Chinese Communist Party, 200n5
Christian morality, 7, 11–12, 108–9;
    Catholic Church, 175; Confucian
    morality v., 50; on evil, 22; moral
    values in, 38–39; televangelists, 175–76,
    180–81; unconditional love, 62, 63;
    Zen Buddhist model v., 62
Cí (parental love), 8
Civilian casualties, 162–63, 164–70; in Iraq,
    200n22
Civil rights movements, 121–23, 129–30
Classical age, 24, 27
Clinton, Bill, 154, 180
Common sense, 19
Communication, moral, 122–23; as
    human rights ally, 122–27; improving
    with age, 90, 94–98, 102; measuring of,
    97–99; rhetoric as, 168, 169; Walzer's

"just" war theory as, 159–64, 171,
    199n13; *see also* Mass media
Conflict, mass media's attention on,
    179–80
Confucian morality, 189n9; *Analects*, 8,
    189n9; Christian model v., 50; Daoist
    view of, 64–65; humanism in, 37; law
    and, 8–11; legal system based on, 9–10;
    Roetz's application of, 194n8; rooted
    in *xiao*, 8–9, 50, 99; "true person" of,
    8, 9; Zeng Zi as exemplar of, 33–34;
    Zhuangzi's negative ethics v., 30–37,
    39, 64–65
Conscience maintenance, 95
Context, moral perspective within, 31–32
Contingency formula, Luhmann's, 116
Contingency, Irony, and Solidarity (Rorty),
    66
Control and power, 33, 38
Cornell, Drucilla, on ethics v. morality, 26
Corporal punishment, 135; *see also*
    Punishment
Courage, 36
Courtroom trials, 148–53
Crazy Horse, 168
Creon, 6–8
Crime and Punishment (Dostoevsky), 71–74
Criminal actions: according to age, 101–2;
    Bernardo, 11–12; Berns, 54–58, 63,
    193n10; Latimer, 10–11
Critique of Practical Reason (Kant), 22, 80,
    175
Croatia, 166
Crying infant, 44–45; *see also* Baby
Cultural invariance, 81–82, 85–86, 95–96

Dahmer, Jeffrey, 131
Dao, 32, 36
Daodejing, 156
Daoism, 5, 32, 36; baby as ideal person, 33,
    101–2, 195n12; Confucian model v.,
    64–65; "doing nothing so that nothing
    remains undone," 29; Kohlberg's
    model v., 99–103; "moral fool" of, 15,
    30, 167, 187; morality of anger v., 64–
    66; negative ethics of, 35–37, 39, 64–
    65; nonhumanism of, 37–39; "old man

Punishment (*continued*)
  Kohlberg's first stage, 95; Kant on,
    83–84, 138–39, 141, 197n18; moral
    and emotional necessity of, 54–55;
    Zimring on death penalty as, 144–47;
    see also Death penalty

Radical, 15
Rasch, William, 107, 195n1
Raskolnikov, Rodion, 72–74
Rationality, 38
Rawls, John, 67, 109; model of fairness,
    114–16
The Reality of the Mass Media (Luhmann),
    172
Reason, 22–23; *Critique of Practical
    Reason*, 80, 175; *Grounding for
    the Metaphysics of Morals*, 80; *The
    Metaphysics of Morals*, 80; *Prolegomena
    to Any Future Metaphysics That Will Be
    Able to Present Itself as Science*, 79–80;
    see also Science
Rector, Ricky, 154
Relativism, ethical, 14–15, 30, 31–32;
    moral awe and, 32; *Zhuangzi's*, 30–37,
    39, 64–65
Religion: Abrahamic, 108; scriptures,
    109–10; separation of state and, 108–9;
    see also specific religion
Ren (goodwill), 34, 36
Responsibility, moral, 22
Revenge, 54; Aristotle on, 55; pain-
    pleasure dialectic behind, 55–56, 58,
    62, 85–86; retributional ethics, 144; *see
    also* Death penalty
Rhetoric (Aristotle), 56; Zen Buddhism v.,
    57–58, 61
Right(s), 50, 52; civil rights movements,
    121–23, 129–30; derivation of, 51;
    European Convention on Human
    Rights, 196n4; fundamentalism and,
    118–19; human, as legal basis, 117–20;
    moral communication as basis for,
    122–27; of prisoners, 134; property, 82,
    83, 85, 111; voting, 125–26; women's,
    117–18, 123–25

Righteous anger, 53–54, 62–63; *see also*
    Anger
Robespierre, Maximilien, 1, 2, 38;
    Kantian morality v., 197n13, 197n16;
    Reign of Terror, 139–40
Roetz, Heiner, 194n8
Romania, 181, 196n1
Rorty, Richard, 66–69, 119; pragmatism
    of, 14–15, 91–92
Russia, 38
Ruth, George Herman, Jr. (Babe Ruth),
    46

Sage, moral, 32–34; Xu You, 64–65, 67,
    75; *Zhuangzi's*, 35–37
Saner, Hans, 29
Scandals, 180–82
Schiff, David, 107, 195n1
Science, 38, 78–79; Bentham's applica-
    tion of, 85–87; empirical evidence,
    62, 78, 81, 86, 94, 97–99; Kant's
    application of, 82–85; Kohlberg's
    application of, 94–98; *Prolegomena
    to Any Future Metaphysics That Will
    Be Able to Present Itself as Science*, 79–
    80
Secularization, of Christian moral values,
    38–39
Self-descriptions, repertoire of, 66
Self-perfection, 67
Self-producing social process, 178–79
Self-referral consciousness, Zen Buddhist
    concern with, 58, 61
Self-righteousness, 33–34
Serbia, 166
Servants, Kant on, 83, 85
Sex: homosexuality, 83, 126, 173, 174,
    176–77; Kant on, 45, 83, 85
Sex and the City, 175, 180
"Shepherd boys" (*Zhuangzi*), 32–33
Shia, 166
Shi Yu (moral exemplar), 33–34
Shun (ancient ruler), 30–34
"Sin," 22; antidote for, 48
Sittlichkeit, 24–25, 26, 27, 189n7
Skepticist position, 29